THE
JEWISH
STATE

THE JEWISH STATE

by

THEODOR HERZL

from the 1917 edition

with a 2014 Foreword by
JEROLD S. AUERBACH

QUID PRO BOOKS
New Orleans, Louisiana

THE JEWISH STATE

Originally published in 1917 by the New York Federation of American Zionists, New York. No copyright is currently claimed in the contents, depictions, or information in this book. Modern format, compilation, and book design copyright © 2014 by Steven Alan Childress. Foreword © 2014 by Jerold S. Auerbach. All rights reserved.

Published in the 2014 reprint edition by Quid Pro Books. This is an unabridged republication of the original 1917 edition of the version entitled *A Jewish State,* 3d ed., trans. Sylvia D'Avigdor, notes and intro., Jacob De Haas (in content similar to the 1904 American printing of the work), itself a translation of *Der Judenstaat,* published in 1896 in Leipzig, Germany, and Vienna, Austria, by Verlags-Buchhandlung.

ISBN 978-1-61027-261-2 (pbk)
ISBN 978-1-61027-260-5 (ebk)

QUID PRO BOOKS
5860 Citrus Blvd.
Suite D-101
New Orleans, Louisiana 70123
www.quidprobooks.com

qp

Cover image based on photograph by Carl Pietzner of Theodor Herzl (1860-1904), as published in *Sport und Salon* circa 1900. Cover design copyright © 2014 by Quid Pro, LLC.

CONTENTS

FOREWORD, 2014, JEROLD S. AUERBACH	i
PREFACE, 1917, JACOB DE HAAS	xv
PREFACE, 1904, JACOB DE HAAS	xvii
PREFACE, 1896, THEODOR HERZL	xxv
INTRODUCTION	1
THE JEWISH QUESTION	11
Previous Attempts at a Solution	13
Causes of Anti-Semitism	14
Effects of Anti-Semitism	16
The Plan	17
Palestine or Argentina?	19
Demand, Medium, Trade	20
Outlines	21
Non-Transferable Goods	22
Purchase of Land	23
Buildings	24
Workmen's Dwellings	24
Unskilled Laborers	25
The Seven-Hours Day	26
The Labor Test	28
Commerce	29
Other Classes of Dwellings	30
Some Forms of Raising Non-Transferable Property	30
Securities of the Company	33
Some of the Company's Functions	35

THE JEWISH STATE

Promotion of Industries	36
Settlement of Skilled Laborers	37
Method of Raising Capital	38
LOCAL GROUPS	43
Our Transmigrations	43
Emigration in Groups	44
Our Ministers	45
Responsible Men of the Local Groups	45
Plans of the Towns	47
The Departure of the Middle Classes	47
The Phenomenon of Multitudes	48
Our Intrinsic Qualities	52
Habits	53
SOCIETY OF JEWS AND JEWISH STATE	55
Negotiorum Gestio	55
The Gestor of the Jews	58
The Occupation of Land	59
Constitution	61
Language	63
Theocracy	64
Laws	64
The Army	64
The Banner	64
Reciprocity and Cartels	65
Benefits of the Emigration of the Jews	66
CONCLUSION	69

FOREWORD

Theodor Herzl and *The Jewish State*

Jerold S. Auerbach

"Inspired by Theodor Herzl's vision of the Jewish State," declared David Ben-Gurion as he read Israel's Proclamation of Independence on May 14, 1948, "the First Zionist Congress proclaimed the right of the Jewish people to national revival in their own country." For better or worse, the modern State of Israel bears slight resemblance to the state that Herzl imagined. But his name is forever linked to the Zionist dream and to its astonishing fulfillment barely fifty years after publication of *The Jewish State*, his slim "pamphlet" as he called it, in 1896.

Herzl seemed a most unlikely advocate of the urgency of national sovereignty in the ancient homeland of the Jewish people after nearly two thousand years of exile and dispersion. Born in Budapest in 1860, he absorbed from his family the core value of the Jewish Enlightenment (*Haskalah*): a yearning for assimilation into modern European society. Once Jews were emancipated from the European ghettos where they had been confined for centuries, they would speak, dress, and behave indistinguishably from the surrounding Christian majority. Above all, they would demonstrate their loyalty to the state and to its rulers.

In 1878 the Herzl family moved to Vienna, where Theodor studied at the university and received a doctorate in law. But playwriting and journalism were more enticing than law practice. By 1894 he had become the Paris correspondent for the respected Vienna *Neue Freie Presse*. It was the perfect geographical and cultural posting for Herzl. A century earlier France had led the way to Jewish emancipation when the National Assembly issued

THE JEWISH STATE

the Declaration of the Rights of Man and of the Citizen, promising freedom and equality to all.

To be sure, during the debate over the eligibility of Jews for French citizenship concern had been expressed lest they continue to exist as "a nation within a nation." The bishop of Nancy wondered: "must one admit into the family a tribe that is a stranger to oneself that constantly turns its eyes toward [another] homeland, that aspires to abandon the land that supports it?" Nonetheless, the new Constitution assured "Liberty to every man to . . . exercise the religious worship to which he is attached." Prominent Jewish leader Berr Isaac Berr pointedly advised fellow Jews of the absolute necessity to "divest ourselves entirely of that narrow spirit . . . in all civil and political matters. . . . We must appear simply as individuals, as Frenchmen, guided only by a true patriotism and by the general good of the nation." Such were the terms of their new freedom that modern Jews eagerly embraced.

In 1894 Theodor Herzl, who passionately believed in the benefits of assimilation that would accompany emancipation, attended the trial of Captain Alfred Dreyfus. A French artillery officer from an assimilated Jewish family, Dreyfus was (falsely) accused of providing secret information to the German government. As Parisian mobs shouted "Death to the Jews," Dreyfus was found guilty and sentenced to life imprisonment on the appropriately named Devil's Island.

Historians and biographers have disagreed over the impact of the Dreyfus trial on Herzl's conversion to Zionism. Scholars long assumed that *The Jewish State*, published two years later, was his impassioned response to the stunning injustice to Dreyfus. But Hebrew University political scientist Shlomo Avineri, Herzl's most recent biographer, disagrees. He notes that Herzl did not link Zionism to the Dreyfus Affair in his diaries or letters. Rather, the clash of national movements within the disintegrating Austro-Hungarian Empire had already convinced him that emancipation provoked, rather than eradicated, anti-Semitism. Reconsidering his assumption that the solution to the Jewish problem could be found in emancipation, Herzl embraced the idea of Jewish statehood that consumed him for the remainder of his life.

Foreword

Herzl was hardly the first modern Jew to offer a national answer to the Jewish Question. Only a decade earlier a group of young Russian Jews known as the Bilu, stunned by a wave of devastating pogroms, proposed Jewish resettlement in the Land of Israel. Jews, they proclaimed, had been "sleeping and dreaming the false dream of assimilation." Now they must awaken from their "charmed sleep" and return to rebuild their ancient homeland.

The pogroms had also provoked Judah Leib Pinsker, a physician born in Russian Poland, to relinquish his diaspora dream of Jewish assimilation and equality. In *Autoemancipation*, published in 1882, Pinsker concluded that "the Jew is nowhere at home, nowhere regarded as a native, he remains an alien everywhere." Emancipation had failed. Pinsker admonished his people: "we must not consent to play forever the hopeless role of the 'Wandering Jew.'" There was only one solution: "the creation of a Jewish nationality, of a people living upon its own soil, the auto-emancipation of the Jews; their return to the ranks of the nations by the acquisition of a Jewish homeland." Within two years Pinsker became a founder of *Hovevei Zion* ("Lovers of Zion"), dedicated to agricultural settlement in the Land of Israel.

Herzl indicated no familiarity with the writings of his Zionist predecessors. It was as though he alone had uncovered the Jewish problem and possessed its solution. No less problematic than his lack of originality—as a reader quickly discerns—was his writing style, which Avineri labels "pompous, bombastic, and theatrical." Yet Herzl achieved what no one else before him had done: with his keen eye for public relations and his flair for dramatic pronouncement, combined with his determination to share his inspiration in encounters with sultans and emperors, he gained world attention for the Zionist idea that culminated in Jewish statehood forty-four years after his premature death in 1904.

Herzl's transformative insight was the durability of anti-Semitism, a consequence of the failure of emancipation. That made a Jewish state, which he envisioned as an "aristocratic republic," essential for Jewish survival. But how could a heterogeneous and widely dispersed people, without a unified national homeland or history for nearly two thousand years, transcend its modern plight of dispersion and the devastating consequences of prejudice and pogroms?

Clearly stunned that a century after emancipation "the world resounds with outcries against the Jews" (perhaps a reference to the Dreyfus Affair), Herzl observed that "the Jewish Question exists wherever Jews live in perceptible numbers." Indeed, Jews carried their misery with them even as they endlessly relocated from country to country in a futile attempt to elude their plight. "We naturally move to those places where we are not persecuted," he lamented, "and there our presence produces persecution."

Herzl perceived the futility of Jewish life in the diaspora. His anguish at the predicament of Jews was palpable: "The nations in whose midst Jews live are all either covertly or openly Anti-Semitic." Not only had emancipation failed to solve the Jewish problem; it had deepened anti-Semitism. "In vain are we loyal patriots," he wrote: "In countries where we have lived for centuries we are still cried down as strangers."

Whether Jews were socialists or capitalists, workers or bankers, they were despised. Because anti-Semitic prejudices "lie deep in the hearts of the people" among whom Jews lived, dreams of assimilation could not be realized. The idea of legal equality, Herzl concluded, had become "a dead letter." Even benevolent rulers could not protect Jews, lest their compassion incur popular wrath. Eerily anticipating the terrifying Nazi demand decades later, Herzl endorsed, for entirely different purposes, what he identified as "that classic Berlin phrase: *'Juden Raus!'*" (Out with the Jews!)

Herzl's response to "the misery of the Jews" emerged from his fundamental insight: "We are one people." Jews, he had come to believe, must be diverted from their consuming quest for integration into their host nations. Their desperate plight could only be alleviated with national sovereignty. The timeless Jewish yearning for "Next Year in Jerusalem" expressed at the conclusion of the Passover Seder must be converted into reality. "We are," Herzl boldly asserted, "strong enough to form a State, and, indeed, a model State."

His plan for implementing that vision—as practical as it was fanciful—comprises the major, and perhaps least compelling, portion of *The Jewish State*. It revealed the mind of an emanci-

Foreword

pated and enlightened Jew who was a supremely rational thinker. But it could not begin to embrace the complexities and passions that the very idea of Jewish statehood inevitably stirred. Jews who remained bound to their religious tradition were prepared to wait patiently for the arrival of the Messiah, not a false messiah from Vienna, to bring redemption. And Jews who wished only to assimilate into the nations they already inhabited were horrified lest a call for Jewish statehood provoke accusations of divided loyalty from within their host societies.

The plan, Herzl wrote, was "perfectly simple": "Let the sovereignty be granted us over a portion of the globe large enough to satisfy the rightful requirements of a nation; the rest we shall manage for ourselves." Once Jews were assured supremacy under international law "over a portion of the globe sufficiently large to satisfy our just requirements," the process of Jewish liberation could begin. He imagined that the governments of nations "scourged by Anti-Semitism" would be "keenly interested" in fostering Jewish national sovereignty, if for no other reason than to encourage their own Jews to depart for their new homeland. He was convinced that Jews "could offer the present possessors of the land enormous advantages"—including assumption of the public debt, building new roads and "many other things," which he did not enumerate. He seemed confident that European rulers would embrace his vision.

Herzl initially suggested Argentina and Palestine as potential locations for a Jewish state. South America offered the advantages of space, a sparse population, and a mild climate. To be sure, the earlier migration of Jews there had already produced "some discontent," which prompted Herzl's confident offer to "enlighten" the local population regarding the differences between ordinary Jews and Zionists. Several years later, near the end of his life, the Kishinev pogroms in Russia prompted him to consider Uganda as an appropriate location for the Jewish national home.

But Herzl certainly understood that "Palestine is our ever-memorable historic home." He imagined that its very name "would attract our people with a force of marvelous potency." Indeed, he suggested: "If His Majesty the Sultan were to give us Palestine, we could in return undertake to regulate the whole

THE JEWISH STATE

finances of Turkey" (thereby reinforcing, ironically, one of the classic stereotypes of Jewish wealth and power). He offered the memorable assurance that Jews in Palestine would "form a portion of a rampart of Europe against Asia, an outpost of civilization as opposed to barbarism."

But how might such a daring proposal be achieved? Reality might be complex, but Herzl's solution was "perfectly simple." He proposed the establishment of two agencies, the Society of Jews and the Jewish Company, to facilitate the relocation of Jews from exile to their promised land. The process, he recognized, would be "gradual, continuous, and will cover many decades." Conceding that "a state is created by a nation's struggle for existence," he nonetheless devoted most of *The Jewish State* to a detailed—indeed, often ponderous—description of how his proposed Society and Company would function.

The Society of Jews would rely upon "scientific methods" to organize the modern exodus. As Herzl acknowledged: "We cannot journey out of Egypt today in the primitive fashion of ancient times." With diversionary references to Rousseau's social contract idea and Papal sovereignty as possible models, he embraced "the theory of rationality" that would provide necessary statistical data to enable the Society to determine "whether the Jews really wish to go to the Promised Land." The Society would launch a scientific study of natural resources, arrange for land distribution and organize a centralized administration. Its representatives, comprising "our keenest thinkers," would be the first to arrive. They would establish universities and technical schools, academies and research institutes.

Eager to minimize the disruption of dislocation, Herzl would delegate responsibility to the Jewish Company for managing the economic aspects of relocation. The basis of independence, he asserted, was private property; the "spirit of enterprise" must be encouraged. Imagining emigration without economic disruption, he foresaw "groups of families and friends," each group accompanied by its own rabbi, making the journey "with the minimum of pain." Should Jews be reluctant to leave their diaspora homes, Herzl was confident that anti-Semites would provide "the requisite impetus."

Foreword

Once the complexities of relocation had been "systematically settled beforehand," Herzl believed, "everything will shape itself quite naturally." In his imagined "aristocratic republic," a council of appointed jurists would draft a constitution (which Israel still lacks after nearly seventy years of national sovereignty). Too much democracy, he warned, produces "objectionable . . . professional politicians" who would mislead the masses.

Herzl recognized that the ingathering of diaspora Jews from many nations, speaking a variety of languages, would pose serious communication problems. "Who amongst us," he famously asked, "has a sufficient acquaintance with Hebrew to ask for a railway ticket in that language?" But Jews must relinquish their "miserable stunted jargons," the "Ghetto languages" that were suitable only for "prisoners." His preferred model was Switzerland's "federation of tongues."

Religion was another touchy subject for Herzl. His dark beard might evoke images of a traditional religious Jew. But from the beginning, his call for a Zionist solution to the Jewish problem had infuriated the European Orthodox rabbinate. Opposed to any form of nationality for a people who "comprise a separate community solely with respect to *religion*," the *Protestrabbiner* had responded furiously to news of the impending first Zionist Congress. Reform and Orthodox rabbis joined together in an unlikely alliance to remind Zionists that Israel's destiny was to become a "kingdom of priests and a holy nation." Eighteen centuries earlier, they asserted, "history made its decision regarding Jewish nationhood through the dissolution of the Jewish State and the destruction of the Temple." Jews were obligated "to serve the country to which they belong with the utmost devotion," not establish their own nation state. Herzl responded in kind. Eager to blunt the emergence of "theocratic tendencies" that might inhibit his plan he preemptively declared: "We shall keep our priests within the confines of their temples."

In the end, Herzl was supremely—some might say blindly—confident that "the Jews, once settled in their own State, would probably have no more enemies." Indeed, he welcomed new arrivals from "other creeds and different nationalities," promising equality before law. After all, he noted sardonically, "We have learnt toleration in Europe." But his proudly optimistic, indeed prophetic, conclusion still resonates: if necessary, the Maccabees "will rise again" to fight for Jewish national freedom.

Herzl rallied Eastern European Jews who sensed in Zionism the possibility of liberation from the prejudice and oppression that tortured their lives. Zionism, he proclaimed, "seeks to secure for the Jewish people a publicly recognized, legally secured, home in Palestine." He boldly called upon the delegates to the First Zionist Congress, whom he summoned to Basle in 1897, "to lay the foundation stone of the house which is to shelter the Jewish nation." They responded to his plea by declaring: "The aim of Zionism is to create for the Jewish people a home in Palestine secured by public law" that would strengthen "Jewish national sentiment and consciousness." Herzl wrote proudly in his diary: "At Basle I founded the Jewish State." In their homeland in Zion, he memorably envisioned, "We shall live at last as free men on our own soil."

Yet Herzl's vision of Jewish national sovereignty, as his sequel to *The Jewish State* revealed, was largely barren of Jewish content. *Altneuland* (Old New Land), published in 1902, offered his imagined future of Zionism in twenty years, once statehood was achieved. In his utopian commonwealth emancipated Jews were all but indistinguishable from the European Christians whose lives and culture they emulated. Residing harmoniously among grateful Arabs who appreciated their civilizing virtues, Jews still looked to the enlightened West, with its "ideas which are the common stock of the whole civilized world," for inspiration. Zionism might reflect Jewish myths and symbols, but the Jewish state that Herzl envisioned was framed within Enlightenment values: "justice, truth, liberty, progress, humanity, and beauty."

Herzl's utopia was a Jewish Vienna without anti-Semitism—or, indeed, Judaism. In *Altneuland*, explained Zionist spokesman David Litwack to a foreign visitor, the "inherited dead-weight" of the Jewish past had finally been lifted. "We only had to take the inventions of the Western world and use them." In their own "New Society," Jews were governed by the laws of "all civilized European countries." No embarrassing questions were asked "about anybody's race or religion."

Foreword

Although lingering traces of Jewish life and culture survived in *Altneuland*, Herzl had little to say about them. During his first visit to Jerusalem in 1898, he had been appalled by the squalor and poverty of the Old City, where Jewish national and religious history had been forged and fused in antiquity. Envisioning its future, he wrote: "I would move the markets elsewhere, and then a new city would be built around the holy places, . . . leaving only houses of prayer and charity institutions within the ancient walls." In the cosmopolitan Jerusalem of *Altneuland*, the home of religious Jews for centuries had been transformed into "an international centre which all nations might regard as their home." In this modern city of "splendid public buildings and places of amusement," an imposing new Temple (barren of Jewish content) was located adjacent to a splendid "Peace Palace" to encourage international harmony. In *Altneuland*, Jews had become a "proud and free" people, if indistinguishable from everyone else, liberated at last to "work for the good of mankind."

Herzl's universalist vision, like his elegant sartorial style (at Basel he had insisted that delegates attending the opening session wear tails and white ties), identified him as a respectable Viennese gentleman yearning for acceptance. He had, after all, once imagined that the Jewish Question, the place of Jews in modern society, could be answered by the mass conversion of Jews to Christianity. *Altneuland* revealed, two years before his death, that Zionism had become his preferred instrument of Jewish acculturation. In their old new homeland Jews, for so long despised ghetto dwellers, had finally been transformed into respectable citizens of the modern world. What newly emancipated Jews had yearned for as individuals—freedom from Judaism and integration into Christian society—*Altneuland* collectively assured to their descendants.

Although Herzl's negotiations with European bankers and Turkish, German, and Russian officials went nowhere, his frustration did not deter him. Convinced that the Jewish people needed a state of their own to survive amid the enticements and perils of modernity, he astutely perceived the solution. Addressing the First Zionist Congress, his diagnosis was unerring. "In these times, so progressive in most respects, we know ourselves to be surrounded by the old, old hatred" of anti-Semitism. Most

THE JEWISH STATE

painfully to Herzl, it even targeted "that very part of Jewry which is modern and cultured, which has outgrown the ghetto"—the part to which Herzl, the emancipated and assimilated Viennese gentleman, belonged. Zionism, he asserted, was "a moral, lawful, humanitarian movement, directed toward the long-yearned-for goal of our people" in their ancient homeland.

Historians and biographers have filled volumes analyzing Theodor Herzl and his Zionist vision. Carl Schorske perceptively observed that Herzl did not propose "a Jewish Utopia, but a liberal one. The dreams of assimilation which could not be realized in Europe would be realized in Zion." To be sure, the problem was not Herzl's alone. More than a century later Zionism remains trapped in the dilemma that Herzl could not resolve: whether Jews, even in Zion, would finally shed the burden of assimilation imposed by emancipation or enthusiastically embrace it and become like everyone else.

Acknowledging Herzl's achievement as "immense and unique," David Vital concludes that "Zionism re-created the Jews as a political nation; and by so doing it revolutionized their collective and private lives." As "the founder of modern Zionism," Amos Elon writes, Herzl "almost single-handedly . . . built and sustained a movement which, within half a century . . . led to the establishment of the modern state of Israel." Anita Shapira, historian of Israel, likens Herzl to "a passing lightning storm that illuminated reality and shook it up, laying the groundwork for future changes." Understanding "the multifaceted character of modern anti-Semitism," he did not permit his embrace of European culture to obscure his penetrating insight that the Jewish problem required a Jewish state for its solution.

As *The Jewish State* and *Altneuland* reveal, Herzl could not resolve the contradictions of Jewish life in modernity. As attracted to nineteenth century utopian socialism as he was to Jewish nationalism, he was pulled between individual and collective values. In *The Jewish State*, his foundation text for Zionism, Herzl's envisioned state would be Jewish in name only; as an aristocratic republic it would lack fundamental democratic institutions. The absence of identifiable Jewish content was perhaps its most conspicuous feature. Yet, as historian Walter Laqueur

Foreword

observed, "Modern political Zionism begins with the publication of *Der Judenstaat*." Whether it would be a Jewish state, or a state of Jews, or both, was left unresolved—and remains so.

More than a century later, the Jewish problem that preoccupied and galvanized Herzl endures. The establishment of a Jewish state came too late for six million Holocaust victims. The legitimacy of Israel as the nation-state of the Jewish people is now challenged worldwide. Diaspora Jews wrestle with their relationship to Israel, whose existence both inspires and complicates their lives. But Herzl's seemingly preposterous vision of Jewish national restoration has been fulfilled.

One year before his death, Herzl requested burial in Vienna "until the Jewish people will transfer my remains to Eretz Israel." In 1949 his wish was fulfilled. Three years later Mt. Herzl became Israel's national cemetery, where leaders of state and fallen soldiers have been buried ever since. There the State of Israel annually celebrates its Independence Day with a torch-lighting ceremony that reaffirms the enduring link between Theodor Herzl's dream of Jewish sovereignty and the reality of Jewish statehood.

JEROLD S. AUERBACH
Professor Emeritus of History
Wellesley College
June 2014

THE JEWISH STATE

AN ATTEMPT AT A MODERN SOLUTION OF THE JEWISH QUESTION

BY

THEODOR HERZL, LL. D.

REVISED FROM THE ENGLISH TRANSLATION OF MISS SYLVIA D'AVIGDOR, WITH SPECIAL PREFACE AND NOTES BY

JACOB DE HAAS

THIRD EDITION

NEW YORK
FEDERATION OF AMERICAN ZIONISTS
1917

PREFACE TO THE EDITION OF 1917

JEWISH STATE

THE demand for a new and cheaper edition of The Jewish State at this time is significant of the growing interest in the ideas first published by Theodor Herzl, in April, 1896. Since the outbreak of the War, in August, 1914, much has happened in the greater world of affairs and within the confines of Jewish life to justify the belief that in writing The Jewish State and organizing the Zionist Movement, Theodor Herzl made a distinct contribution to the political idealism of the Nineteenth Century.

After mature consideration, it seems advisable to allow the preface of 1904 to stand, for it checks up the accomplishments toward the realization of The Jewish State from its publication in 1896 to February, 1904. Much has happened since which would demand more than a prefatory note to describe. Suffice, then, to say that all that which had to be done to refurbish what was accomplished up to 1904 has been done between 1914 and 1917. The Zionist ground had been more than recovered, and it is safe to suggest that the hopes for the restoration of Israel to Palestine, which at this time is one of the commonplaces of public discussion, will, in all probability, be achieved in form as well as in substance along the lines foreshadowed by Theodor Herzl.

June 1, 1917.

JACOB DE HAAS.

EDITOR'S PREFACE TO THE EDITION OF 1904

THOUGH proportionately heretofore but little read or studied, the pages that follow this introduction will eventually occupy a noteworthy place in Jewish and universal history. Whilst the author, Dr. Theodor Herzl, was, confessedly, not moved by the novelty of the Jewish State idea, yet he was in the main unconscious in the winter of 1895 of the parentage of his thoughts; for those who had labored before him, excepting George Eliot, were comparatively obscure, and their words had only found acceptance amongst eclectic bands of enthusiasts in Eastern Europe. It is, however, curious that though argumentative, polemical or enthusiastic, none of the forerunners of the Jewish State were, in the real sense, visionaries; and this brochure is only grandiose in the simplicity of its presentation of an idea, and historic by what its publication has already achieved. Though the Jewish State idea may be Utopian, which its advocates deny, its author sketched no Utopia, and offers no picture of an ideal human future—it was sufficient for him to point out how the wounds of Israel might be healed and to remove the chafing which the conjunction of Jew and anti-Semite brings about. He offered a temporal and not a spiritual salvation to a suffering people, though those who regard him as thereby doing an allotted task towards a destiny divinely decreed, are not without reasonable justification for their opinion.

The Jewish position became so critical in 1890 that Baron de Hirsch thought out his Argentine plans, and began founding his colonies, in the pampas grass districts of the Spanish-American Republic, in order to aid the Jews to remove themselves from persecuted countries.

The rise of Ahlwardt in Germany, the break-up of the Liberal party in Austria, and the particular success of the anti-Semitic factions in Vienna, the trial and sentence of Dreyfus in Paris, and

THE JEWISH STATE

the immediate lowering of the position of the Jews in France which followed, and for which Drumont had labored partially, the failure of the Argentine experiments—these facts, and others of lesser and greater degree will mark out the first half of the last decade of the nineteenth century as black years in Jewish history. It was seeing and hearing these things, as an observer rather than as a participant, that Theodor Herzl came to the Jewish people with an old thought, "We are a people—one people," and an old corollary, "The restoration of the Jewish State"; unaware that, except in a vague way, there was at least fifteen years of active work, and some propaganda behind him. Fearful, perhaps, of being regarded as a visionary, he vaguely designated the land of the future Jewish State simply as "over there." And "over there" it would undoubtedly have remained had not the "Jewish State" responded to a thought, definite and concise, long pent up in Jewish bosoms. "Over there" must be Palestine. Herzl, as a cool thinker, argued that the propelling force needed to create a Jewish State exists in the misery of the Jews. The volume of that misery is unmistakable; but his book was taken up by and his following was created out of an element who, though in close touch with misery, often the actual sufferers, found within themselves a still greater motive power to national restoration than misery: to wit, love, faith and hope, a bundle of emotions wrapped in the praying shawl of the Jew; and these, when spread out, make up a flag which can only float in the breezes of Zion.

This "Jewish State," therefore, went through such violent natal sufferings as only great ideas suffer. The very fact that on this vision of a Jewish State, other visionaries wrote yet a more cloudy word: Palestine, was sufficient to condemn it in the eyes of most Western Jews. They had from the beginning of the century, in the endeavor to reconcile old Judaism with modern life, passed through several phases, sometimes concurrently, sometimes separated and distinct from each other,—spirituality, assimilation and science (Judaism is again being reduced to knowledge) in all of which the Palestinian and the one people theories were absent, obliterated and often forgotten. The Jews had become a religious community, and Judaism a religion with an extensive ritual. As a Western Jew, Herzl was a freak; his book, except as the dream of an idle moment—intolerable, and as a political suggestion,

Preface

unthinkable and absurd. A popular verdict was that it was an "egregious blunder," notwithstanding which, the masses being brought into touch with the author, listened and approved. For the first time in modern history the Jewish masses—it was the first opportunity given them—began to move of their own accord. And the author of a political plan became, in a day and a night, the leader of a Jewish party, which decided to use modern methods to attain their goal—Palestine. Rabbis might proclaim every city as Zion; the rich might frown and refuse support—the modern Zionist movement "leapt full bodied into being," and asserted its existence six months after the author had spoken face to face with the "poor and lowly," who offered him at once their loyalty and their enthusiasm, and who, linking his profession as writer to his doctrine as Jew, regarded him as a new Ezra.

Dr. David Kaufmann, in his notable criticism of "Daniel Deronda" in 1879, observed: "Feelings and sentiments which are worthy to be cherished and preserved in the nation's soul against all the influences of time are wont to concentrate themselves in great personalities, and to impart to them a power of attraction before which moderation and half-heartedness fly like leaves before the storm. The history of Israel presents a number of such figures. Ezra and Nehemiah succeed to the Prophets of the Captivity; John of Giskala stands beside Judas Maccabæus; Akiba ben Joseph defends the Star-Son of Bethar, and even through the darkness of the middle ages the fiery pillar of Jehudah ben Levi gleams forth. Shall we some day be able to say—'and so on?'" The Jewish masses, whose greatness is that they have miraculously conserved an ideal, answered this question by acclaiming Theodor Herzl as leader of the Jewish national movement.

And from the moment he was so acclaimed, the Jewish State had ceased to be a paper plan; indeed, the brochure had no circulation commensurate with its effect—but it had made a page of Jewish history. Between the printed word and its objective are eight remarkable years of history; the story of the reuniting of the elements of the Diaspora; the creation of a Jewish public opinion; the organization of unwieldy and widely separated masses, largely ignorant of the methods of modern political life; political negotiations, and finally political recognition by the Great Powers of the loyalty, utility and representative character of the movement—it is the story of another Exodus with Israel still in the wilderness.

Those who read the "Jewish State" on its first appearance, either rejected its teachings, or accepted them with the eye of hope. Those who will now read it for the first time will probably be guided by the answer that is given to the question, "What has been accomplished in the direction of a 'Jewish State' since this book—for which a niche in history is claimed—first appeared?" And it is because of that question that this preface has been written. A brief chronological table will supply the outline of the answer.

    1896, April—Publication of English edition of "Jewish State."

    1896, June—Dr. Herzl visits Constantinople; on return journey received at Sofia a deputation of Bulgarian Jews.

    1896, July—Dr. Herzl addresses East London mass meeting.

    1897, January—Founding of Zionist organ, "Die Welt."

    1897, February—Proposal to call Congress in Munich; rabbis protest.

    1897, March—Zionist Congress convened at Basle.

    1897, August—First Zionist Congress held, at which the national platform was adopted:

        "The aim of Zionism is to create for the Jewish people a publicly legally assured home in Palestine.

        "In order to attain this the Congress adopts the following means:

(1) To promote the settlement in Palestine of Jewish agriculturists, handicraftsmen, industrialists and those following professions.

(2) The centralization of the entire Jewish people by means of general institutions, agreeably to the laws of the land.

(3) To strengthen Jewish sentiments and national self-consciousness.

(4) To obtain the sanction of governments to the carrying out of the objects of Zionism."

    1898, August—Second Zionist Congress held, at which it was resolved to found Zionist bank.

    1898, November—Dr. Herzl and Zionist deputation received by the German Emperor at Jerusalem.

    1899, August—Third Zionist Congress held.

Preface

1900, August—Fourth Zionist Congress held in London, and stability of Jewish Colonial Trust as a banking concern assured.

1901, May—Dr. Herzl repeatedly received in audience by the Sultan of Turkey.

1901, December—Fifth Zionist Congress held; scheme of organization remodelled, and Jewish National Fund founded.

1902, January—Dr. Herzl again received in audience by Sultan of Turkey.

1902, August—Dr. Herzl appears as witness before British Royal Commission on Alien Immigration.

1902, August—Dr. Herzl again received in audience by Sultan of Turkey.

1903, January—British Government offer, and expedition is sent to El Arisch, on the Egyptian border of Palestine.

1903, July—Dr. Herzl received by M. von Plehve and M. de Witte on behalf of the Russian Government.

1903, August—Sixth Zionist Congress held, and offer from the British Government to permit Jewish national settlement in British East Africa.

1904, February—Dr. Herzl received in audience by the King of Italy and the Pope.

Even in the bald form of a chronological table, it is evident that the record of those who hearkened to the "Jewish State" idea is a notable one, sufficient to claim the sympathy and support of every Jew and Jewess. The book was moulded into the platform of 1897, in the framing of which more than one cautious brain had a share; and in turn the question arises in how far has this program become living fact. A comparison of these facts and the author's idea will show that, in as far as he shaped the movement, he was most tenacious of his ideas. The work has proceeded much on the lines he suggested, this perhaps by reason of their simplicity—for much that has made the Zionist movement grew up and around him. Those who joined Theodor Herzl in the effort to realize his plan brought with them the instincts, hopes and desires of the Jewish people, thoughts and ideals red with the blood that gave them birth, truer and more significant of that which is eternal in each people than all that the study and the school room can

THE JEWISH STATE

suggest. A stupendous work awaited those who proclaimed Palestine, as the third part of the thought, one people—national Jewish restoration. Only the most rudimentary scheme of organization was established in 1897, yet it called forth so much enthusiasm that it has been twice revised in accordance with the growing needs of a movement that actually circles the globe, an organization which is at once centripetal and centrifugal, and yet has in each country to correspond with the social customs of the people and keep within the laws that restrict international and even national organization in Eastern Europe. Here alone is a task for a generation, and room for the brains of the most able organizers. Yet all the rough work has been done, and the second clause of the program has been fulfilled at comparatively no expense.

The self-volition of the movement checked the assimilative thought and revived the Jewish brotherhood idea; the "bent back" of the Jew grew straight in the presence of the Jewish flag; a new poetry and a new prosody, deep with the feelings that stir a people, have arisen; a school of young artists have given themselves over to the creation of a Jewish art; others have planned an international Jewish university; a cultural movement—combated for the time being by the more orthodox—has spread so strongly as sometimes to shake the main movement from its true centre; the Hebrew tongue has found need and occasion to blossom into a living language; and with the national, intellectual renaissance—which sweeps within itself the revival of conservative Jewish thought, which is the present phase of American Jewish life—has come a desire for the development of the physical powers of the Jews, so that Jewish gymnasiums and Jewish gymnastic journals exist to the surprise of all those who know the Jew only as a brainy creature. The thousand facets of a national movement have sent rays of light, of hope, and of a new sense of security into the lives of an erstwhile broken and dispirited people. In eight short years helpless masses have been so well taught how human effort can accomplish great things that they have rejected the possibilities of immediate aid in favor of the task of striving for independent life. A distracted and divided people have been so well instructed in the thought that the unity of Israel is greater than all the differing religious, social, economic and political views of the individuals

Preface

who make up a nation, that the Rabbis of Eastern Europe have entered in full force into the vanguard of the movement. The third clause of the program has been literally fulfilled, though much remains to be done.

Palestine has not been repeopled; the settlement of colonists has been checked rather than assisted, because the condition of settlement is governed by the preamble of the platform. Nevertheless, a new spirit has manifested itself in Palestine, as well in the minds of those who have dealt with the practical administration of the colonies, and a Zionist bank has been started in Jaffa, which is already giving an impetus to Palestinian trade. That which interests the majority who would like to weld all the details into broad achievement is contained in the fourth paragraph. "The sanction of the governments" has been gradually obtained. The German Emperor was the first to express his "benevolent attitude"; French and English ministers have listened with sympathy; the King of Italy has approved; the Pope has discussed; the Sultan of Turkey has repeatedly sent for Dr. Herzl. The negotiations were inconclusive, but since the last known phase of the Constantinople pourparlers the British and Russian governments publicly recognized Zionism; and the latter offered to assist in the Palestinian negotiations when resumed. From paper plan to this stage is a remarkable achievement in eight years, and the strongest opponent of the cause, the London *Jewish Chronicle,* affirmed in September, 1903, that in its opinion "the creation of a Jewish State in Palestine is now the settled policy of European statesmen, who are dealing with the near Eastern question."

Far be it from one who has abiding faith in the Jewish democracy to ascribe all these things to one man and one book. The living element in a people has forced an old thought upon a new world; and such an element, ever young in its hopes and effort, will continue to force it upon the consciousness of an ever new world, until one generation shall witness the triumph of this idea. Theodor Herzl revived and reorganized the Jewish people. This is his achievement and the message of his book. It caught its echoes from the ages that preceded its writing, and it will ring on into new born days in an ever-accumulating volume of sound; the message is—the union of Israel and Zion.

THE JEWISH STATE

* * * *

Since the foregoing was written, Theodor Herzl, man and leader, has passed away, and this publication of his first Zionist writing becomes a tribute to his memory. His death has proved his life's work—he built beyond himself—and his demise is but a consecration and a sanctification of Zionism. The manner of the man, the life he led, all this is written elsewhere. In these pages will be found, as it were, his testament, his thought modified by the conditions of its nationalization, and, it is the thought, the hope, the regenerative idea, which is Theodor Herzl's bequest to Israel.

JACOB DE HAAS.

New York, Tammuz 25, 5664.

AUTHOR'S PREFACE

THE IDEA which I have developed in this pamphlet is a very old one: the restoration of the Jewish State.

The earth resounds with outcries against the Jews, and these outcries have awakened the slumbering idea.

I wish it to be clearly understood from the outset that no portion of my argument is based on a new discovery. I have discovered neither the historic condition of the Jews nor the means to improve it. In fact, every man will see for himself that the materials of the structure I am designing are not only in existence, but actually ready to hand. If, therefore, this attempt to solve the Jewish Question is to be designated by a single word, let it be called a "combination," certainly not a "phantasy."

I must, in the first place, guard my scheme from being treated as Utopian by superficial critics who might commit this error of judgment if I did not warn them. I should obviously have done nothing to be ashamed of, if I had described a Utopia on philanthropic lines; and I should also, in all probability, have obtained literary success more easily if I had set forth my plan in the irresponsible guise of a romantic tale.* But this Utopia is far less attractive than any one of those portrayed by Sir Thomas More and his numerous forerunners and successors. And I believe that the situation of the Jews in many countries is grave enough to make preliminary trifling superfluous.

An interesting book—"Freiland," by Dr. Theodor Hertzka— which appeared a few years ago, may serve to mark the distinction I draw between my conception and a Utopian one. His is the ingenious invention of a modern mind thoroughly schooled in the

---

* He subsequently did so in "Altneuland." — De Haas [by the editor, as with all footnotes added to the remaining text, and bracketed inserts in the text].

principles of political economy, and is as remote from actuality as the Equatorial mountain on which his dream State lies. "Freiland" is a complicated piece of mechanism with numerous cogged wheels catching into each other; but there is nothing to prove that they can be set in motion. Even supposing "Freiland societies" were to come into existence, I should look on the whole thing as a joke.

The scheme in question, on the other hand, includes the employment of an existent propelling force. In consideration of my own inadequacy, I shall content myself with indicating the cogs and wheels of the machine to be constructed, and shall rely on more skilled mechanics than myself to put them together.

Everything depends on our propelling force. And what is our propelling force? The misery of the Jews.

Who would venture to deny its existence? We shall discuss it fully in the chapter on the causes of Anti-Semitism.

Everybody is familiar with the phenomenon of steam-power, generated by boiling water, lifting the kettle-lid. Such tea-kettle phenomena are the attempts of Zionists and of kindred associations to check Anti-Semitism.

Now I believe that this power, if rightly employed, is powerful enough to propel a large engine and to despatch passengers and goods; the engine having whatever form men may choose to give it.

I am absolutely convinced that I am right—though I doubt whether I shall live to see myself proved to be so. Those who are the first to inaugurate this movement will scarcely live to see its glorious close. But the inauguration of it is enough to give them self-respect and the joy of freedom of soul.

I shall not be lavish in artistically elaborated descriptions of my project, for fear of incurring the suspicion of painting a Utopia. I anticipate, in any case, that thoughtless scoffers will caricature my sketch and thus try to weaken its effect. A Jew, intelligent in other respects, to whom I explained my plan, was of opinion that "a Utopia was a project whose future details were represented as already extant." This is a fallacy. Every Chancellor of the Exchequer calculates in his estimate with suppositious figures, and not only with such as are based on the average returns of past years, or

Preface

on previous revenues in other States, but sometimes with figures for which there is no precedent whatever; as, for example, in instituting a new tax. Everybody who studies a Budget knows that this is the case. But even if it were known that the estimate would not be rigidly adhered to, would the new system of administration be therefore considered Utopian?

But I am forming greater expectations of my readers. I ask the cultivated men whom I am addressing to set many preconceived ideas entirely aside. I shall even go so far as to ask those Jews who have most earnestly tried to solve the Jewish Question, to look upon their previous attempts as mistaken and futile.

I must guard against a danger in setting forth my idea. If I describe future circumstances with too much caution, I shall appear to doubt of their possibility. If, on the other hand, I announce their realization with too much assurance, I shall appear to be describing a chimera.

I will therefore clearly and emphatically state that I believe in the practical outcome of my scheme, though without professing to have discovered the shape it may ultimately take. The Jewish State is essential to the world; it will therefore be created.

The plan would, of course, seem absurd if a single individual attempted to work it; but if worked by a number of Jews in cooperation, it would appear perfectly rational, and its accomplishment would present no insurmountable difficulties. The idea depends only on the number of its supporters. Perhaps those ambitious young men, to whom every road of progress is now closed, seeing in this Jewish State a bright prospect of freedom, happiness, and honors opening to them, will ensure the propagation of the idea.

I feel that with the publication of this pamphlet my task is done. I shall not again take up the pen, unless the attacks of noteworthy antagonists drive me to do so, or it becomes necessary to meet unforeseen objections and to remove errors.

Am I stating what is not yet the case? Am I before my time? Are the sufferings of the Jews not yet grave enough? We shall see.

Now it depends on the Jews to make of this either a political pamphlet or a political romance. If the present generation is too dull to understand it rightly, a future, a finer, and a better generation will arise to understand it. The Jews wish for a State—they shall have it, and they shall earn it for themselves.

THE JEWISH STATE

THE JEWISH STATE

INTRODUCTION

IT IS astonishing how little insight many of the men who move in the midst of active life possess of the science of economics. Hence it is that even Jews faithfully repeat the cry of the Anti-Semites: "We depend for sustenance on the nations whose guests we are, and if we had not hosts to support us we should die of Starvation." This is a point that shows how greatly unjust accusations may weaken our self-knowledge. But what are the true grounds for this statement concerning the nations which take us in? Where it is not based on limited physiocratic views it is founded on the childish error that commodities pass from hand to hand in continuous rotation. We need not wake from long slumber, like Rip van Winkle, to realize that the world is considerably altered by the production of new commodities. The technical progress made during this wonderful era enables even a man of most limited intelligence to note with his short-sighted eyes the appearance of innumerable new commodities. The spirit of enterprise has created them.

Labor without enterprise is the stationary labor of ancient days; and typical of it is the work of the husbandman, who stands now just where his progenitors stood a thousand years ago. All our material welfare has been brought about by men of enterprise. I feel almost ashamed of writing down so trite a remark. Even if we were a nation of promoters—such as absurdly exaggerated accounts make us out to be—we should not require another nation to live on. We do not depend only on the circulation of old commodities, because we produce new ones.

We possess slaves of extraordinary strength for work, whose appearance in the world has been fatal to the production of handmade goods: these slaves are the machines. It is true that workmen are required to set machinery in motion; but for this we have men in plenty, in superabundance. Only those who are ignorant of the condition of Jews in many countries of Eastern Europe would venture to assert that Jews are either unfit or unwilling to perform manual labor.

But I do not wish to take up the cudgels for the Jews in this pamphlet. It would be useless. Everything rational and everything sentimental that can possibly be said in their defence, has been said already. New arguments in favor of a certain condition of mind or of feeling answer no purpose. If one's hearers are incapable of comprehending them, one is a preacher in a desert. And if one's hearers are broad and high-minded enough to have grasped them already, then the whole sermon is superfluous. I believe in the Ascent of man to higher and yet higher grades of civilization; but I consider this ascent to be desperately slow. Were we to wait till average humanity had become as charitably inclined as was Lessing when he wrote "Nathan the Wise," we should wait beyond our day, beyond the days of our children, of our grand-children and of our great-grandchildren. But the world spirit comes to our aid in another way.

This century has given the world a wonderful renaissance by means of its technical acquisitions; but at the same time its miraculous improvements have not been employed in the service of humanity. Distance has ceased to be an obstacle, yet we complain of insufficient space. Our great steamships carry us swiftly and surely over hitherto unvisited seas. Our railways carry us safely into a mountain-world heretofore tremblingly scaled on foot. Events occurring in countries undiscovered when Europe confined the Jews in Ghettos, are known to us in the course of an hour. Hence the misery of the Jews is an anachronism—not because there was a period of enlightenment one hundred years ago, for that enlightenment reached in reality only the choicest spirits.

Now, I am of opinion that electric light was not invented for the purpose of illuminating the drawing-rooms of a few snobs, but rather for the purpose of throwing light on some of the dark problems of humanity. One of these problems, and not the least of them, is the Jewish question. In solving it, we are working not only

Introduction

for ourselves, but for many other over-burdened and oppressed beings also.

The Jewish question still exists. It would be useless to deny it. It is a remnant of the Middle Ages, which civilized nations do not even yet seem able to shake off, try as they will. They certainly showed a generous desire to do so when they emancipated us. The Jewish question exists wherever Jews live in perceptible numbers. Where it does not exist, it is carried by Jews in the course of their migrations. We naturally move to those places where we are not persecuted, and there our presence produces persecution. This is the case in every country, and will remain so, even in those most highly civilized—France itself being no exception—till the Jewish question finds a solution on a political basis. The unfortunate Jews are now carrying Anti-Semitism into England; they have already introduced it into America.

I believe that I understand Anti-Semitism, which is really a highly complex movement. I consider it from a Jewish standpoint, yet without fear or hatred. I believe that I can see what elements there are in it of vulgar sport, of common trade jealousy, of inherited prejudice, of religious intolerance, and also of pretended self-defence. I think the Jewish question is no more a social than a religious one, notwithstanding that it sometimes takes these and other forms. It is a national question, which can only be solved by making it a political world-question to be discussed and controlled by the civilized nations of the world in council.

We are a people—One people.

We have honestly endeavored everywhere to merge ourselves in the social life of surrounding communities, and to preserve only the faith of our fathers. It has not been permitted to us. In vain are we loyal patriots, our loyalty in some places running to extremes; in vain do we make the same sacrifices of life and property as our fellow citizens; in vain do we strive to increase the fame of our native land in science and art, or her wealth by trade and commerce. In countries where we have lived for centuries we are still cried down as strangers, and often by those whose ancestors were not yet domiciled in the land where Jews had already made experience of suffering. The majority may decide which are the strangers; for this, as indeed every point which arises in the commerce of nations, is a question of might. I do not here surrender any portion of our prescriptive right, for I am making this statement merely in my own name as an individual. In the world of today, and for an indefinite period it will probably remain so, might precedes right. Therefore it is useless for us to be loyal patriots, as were the Huguenots who were forced to emigrate. If we could only be left in peace. . . .

But I think we shall not be left in peace.

Oppression and persecution cannot exterminate us. No nation on earth has survived such struggles and sufferings as we have gone through. Jew-baiting has merely stripped off our weaklings; the strong among us were invariably true to their race when persecution broke out against them. This attitude was most clearly apparent in the period immediately following the emancipation of the Jews. Later on, those who rose to a higher degree of intelligence and to a better worldly position lost their communal feeling to a very great extent. Wherever our political well-being has lasted for any length of time, we have assimilated with our surroundings. I think this is not discreditable. Hence, the statesman who would wish to see a Jewish strain in his nation would have to provide for the duration of our political well-being; and even Bismarck could not do that.

For old prejudice against us still lies deep in the hearts of the people. He who would have proofs of it need only listen to the people where they speak with frankness and simplicity: proverb and fairy-tale are both Anti-Semitic. A nation is a great child, which can certainly be educated; but its education would, even in most favorable circumstances, occupy such a vast amount of time that we could, as already mentioned, remove our own difficulties by other means long before the process was accomplished.

Assimilation, which implies, in addition to external conformity in dress, habits, customs, and language, identity also of feeling and manner—assimilation of Jews could only be effected by intermarriage. But the need for mixed marriages would have to be felt by the majority; their mere recognition by law would certainly not suffice. The Hungarian Liberals, who have just given legal

Introduction

sanction to mixed marriages,* have made a remarkable mistake, which one of the earliest cases clearly illustrates; a baptized Jew married a Jewess. At the same time the struggle to obtain the present form of marriage accentuated distinctions between Jews and Christians, thus hindering rather than aiding the fusion of races. Those who really wish to see the Jews disappear through intermixture with other nations can only hope to see it come about in one way. The Jews must previously acquire economic power sufficiently great to overcome all social prejudice against them. The aristocracy may serve as an example of this, for in its ranks occur the proportionately largest numbers of mixed marriages. The Jewish families which regild the old nobility with their coin, become gradually absorbed. But what shape would this phenomenon take in the middle classes, where (the Jews being a bourgeois people) the Jewish question is of far more consequence? A previous acquisition of power would be synonymous with that economic supremacy which Jews are already erroneously declared to possess. And if the power they now possess creates rage and indignation among the Anti-Semites, what outbreaks would not an increase of power create? Hence the first step towards absorption will never be taken, because this step would involve the subjection of the majority to a heretofore scorned minority, possessing neither military nor administrative force of its own. I think, therefore, that the absorption of Jews by means of their prosperity is unlikely to occur. In countries which are now Anti-Semitic my view will be approved. In countries where Jews are now tolerated, it will probably be violently disputed. My happier co-religionists will not believe me till Jew-baiting teaches them the truth; for the longer Anti-Semitism lies in abeyance the more fiercely will it break out. The infiltration of immigrating Jews, attracted to a land by apparent security, and the ascent in the social scale of rising Jews, combine powerfully to bring about a revolution. Nothing is plainer than this rational conclusion.

 Because I have drawn this conclusion with complete indifference to everything but the quest of truth, I shall probably be contradicted and opposed by Jews who are in easy circumstances. In so far as private interests alone are held by their anxious

---

* 1895.

possessors to be in danger, they can safely be ignored, for the concerns of the poor and oppressed are of greater importance than theirs. But I wish from the outset to prevent any misconception from arising, particularly the mistaken notion that my project, if realized, would in the least degree injure property now held by Jews. I shall therefore explain everything connected with rights of property, very fully. Whereas, if my plan never becomes anything more than a piece of literature, things will merely remain as they were.

It might more reasonably be objected that I am giving a handle to Anti-Semitism when I say we are a people—One people; that I am hindering the assimilation of Jews, where it is about to be consummated, and endangering it where it is an accomplished fact, in so far as it is possible for a solitary writer to hinder or endanger anything.

This objection will be especially brought forward in France. It will probably also be made in other countries, but I shall answer only the French Jews beforehand, because these afford the most striking example of my point.

However much I may worship individuality—powerful personal individuality in statesmen, inventors, artists, philosophers, or commanders, as well as conjoint individuality in a historic group of human beings, which we call a nation—however much I may worship individuality, I do not regret its disappearance. Whatever is unfit to survive can, will, and must be destroyed. But the distinctive nationality of Jews neither can, will, nor must be destroyed. It cannot be destroyed, because external enemies consolidate it.* It will not be destroyed: this it has shown during 2000 years of appalling suffering. It must not be destroyed, and that, as successor to numberless Jews who refused to despair, I am trying once more to prove in this pamphlet. Whole branches of Judaism may wither and fall, but the trunk remains.

---

* Answering Major Evans Gordon, before the British Royal Commission on Alien Immigration in August, 1902, Dr. Herzl said: "I will give you my definition of a nation, and you can add the adjective 'Jewish.' A nation is, in my mind, a historical group of men of a recognizable cohesion held together by a common enemy. That is in my view a nation. Then if you add to that the word 'Jewish' you have what I understand to be the Jewish nation.

Introduction

Hence, if all or any of the French Jews protest against this scheme on account of their own "assimilation," my answer is simple: The whole thing does not concern them at all. They are Jewish Frenchmen, well and good! This is a private affair for the Jews alone.

The movement towards the organization of the State I am proposing would, of course, harm Jewish Frenchmen no more than it would harm the "assimilated" of other countries. It would, on the contrary, be distinctly to their advantage. For they would no longer be disturbed in their "chromatic function," as Darwin puts it, but would be able to assimilate in peace, because Anti-Semitism, now active, would have been stopped for ever. They would certainly be credited with being assimilated to the very depths of their souls, if they stayed where they were after the Jewish State, with its superior organization, had become a reality.

"Assimilated" would profit even more than Christian citizens by the departure of faithful Jews; for they would be rid of the disquieting, incalculable, and unavoidable rivalry of a Jewish proletariat, driven by poverty and political pressure from place to place, from land to land. This floating proletariat would become stationary. Many Christian citizens—whom we call Anti-Semites—can now offer determined resistance to the immigration of foreign Jews. Jewish citizens cannot do this, although it affects them far more nearly; for on them tells first of all the keen competition of Individuals carrying on similar branches of industry, who, in addition, either introduce Anti-Semitism where it does not exist, or intensify it where it does. The "assimilated" give expression to this secret grievance in "philanthropic undertakings." They found emigration societies for wandering Jews. There is a reverse to the picture which were comic, if it did not deal with human beings. For these charitable institutions are created not for, but against, persecuted Jews—are created to despatch these poor creatures just as fast and as far as possible. And thus, many an apparent friend of the Jews turns out, on careful inspection, to be nothing more than an Anti-Semite of Jewish origin disguised in the garb of a philanthropist.

But the attempts at colonization made even by really benevolent men, interesting attempts though they were, have so far been unsuccessful. I do not think that one man or another took up the matter merely as an amusement; that they allowed poor Jews to migrate, as a herd of cattle might have been let go. The matter was too grave and tragic for such treatment. These attempts were interesting, in that they represented on a small scale the practical forerunners of the idea of a Jewish State. They were useful, in that out of their mistakes may be gathered experience for carrying them out successfully on a larger scale. They have, of course, done harm also. The transportation of Anti-Semitism to new districts, which is the inevitable consequence of such artificial infiltration, seems to me to be the least of these evils. Far worse is the circumstance that unsatisfactory results tend to cast doubts on the efficacy of Jewish labor. But the following simple argument will remove this doubt from the minds of intelligent men. What is inefficacious, and impossible to accomplish on a small scale, need not necessarily be so on a larger one. A small enterprise may result in loss under the same conditions which would make a large one pay. A rivulet cannot even be navigated by boats, the river into which it flows carries fine iron vessels.

No human being is wealthy or powerful enough to transplant a nation from one habitation to another. An idea alone can compass that; and this idea of a State may have the requisite power to do so. The Jews have dreamed this kingly dream all through the long nights of their history. "Next year in Jerusalem" is their old phrase. Now comes the opportunity to prove that the dream may be converted into a living reality.

For this, many old, outgrown, confused and limited notions must first be entirely erased from the minds of men. Dull brains might, for instance, imagine that this exodus would be from civilized regions into the desert. That is not the case. It will be carried out in the midst of civilization. We shall not revert to a lower stage; we shall rise to a higher one. We shall not dwell in mud huts; we shall build newer and more beautiful houses, and possess them in safety. We shall not lose our acquired possessions; we shall realize them. We shall surrender our well-earned rights only for greater privileges. We shall not sacrifice our beloved customs; we shall find them again. We shall not leave our old home before the new is prepared for us. Those only will depart who are sure thereby to improve their position; those who are now

Introduction

desperate will go first, after them the poor; next the prosperous, and, last of all, the opulent. The precursors will raise themselves to a higher grade, equal to that class whose representatives will shortly follow. Thus the exodus will be at the same time an ascent of the classes.

The departure of the Jews will involve no economic disturbances, no crises, no persecutions; in fact, the countries they abandon will revive to a new period of prosperity. There will be an inner migration of Christian citizens into the positions evacuated by Jews. The outgoing current will be gradual and continuous, and its initial movement will put an end to Anti-Semitism. The Jews will leave as honored friends, and if some of them return, they will receive the same favorable welcome and treatment at the hands of civilized nations as is accorded to all foreign visitors. Their exodus will have no resemblance to a flight, for it will be a well-regulated expedition under control of public opinion. The movement will not only be inaugurated with absolute conformity to law, but it cannot even be carried out without the friendly intervention of interested Governments, who would derive considerable benefits from it.

Security for the integrity of the idea and the vigor of its execution will be found in the creation of a body corporate, or corporation. This corporation will be called "The Society of Jews." In addition to it there will be a Jewish Company, a self-supporting, paying body.

An individual who attempted even to undertake this huge task alone might be either an impostor or a madman. The personal characters of the members of the corporation will guarantee its integrity, and the business capital of the Company will prove its stability.

These prefatory remarks are merely intended as a hasty reply to the crowd of objections which the very words "Jewish State" are certain to arouse. Henceforth we shall proceed more slowly to meet further objections and to explain in detail what has been as yet only indicated; and we shall try in the interests of this pamphlet to avoid making it a dull exposition. Short aphoristic chapters will therefore best answer the purpose.

If I wish to substitute a new building for an old one, I must demolish before I construct. I shall therefore keep to this natural sequence. In the first and general part I shall explain my ideas, remove all prejudices, determine essential political and economic conditions, and develop the plan.

In the special part, which is divided into three principal sections, I shall describe its execution. These three sections are: The Jewish Company, Local Groups, and the Society of Jews. The Society is to be created first, the Company last; but in this account the reverse order is preferable, because it is the financial soundness of the enterprise which will chiefly be called into question, and doubts on this score must be removed first.

In the conclusion, I shall try to meet every further objection that could possibly be made. My Jewish readers will, I hope, follow me patiently to the end. Some will naturally make their objections in an order of succession other than that chosen for their refutation. But whoever sees his doubts set aside ought to give in his allegiance to the cause.

Although I speak of reason, I am fully aware that reason alone will not suffice. Old prisoners do not willingly leave their cell. And we shall see whether the young, whom we need, have grown up to us; whether the young, who irresistibly draw on the old, will transform rational motives into enthusiasm.

THE JEWISH QUESTION

NO ONE can deny the gravity of the Jews' situation. Wherever they live in perceptible numbers, they are more or less persecuted. Their equality before the law, granted by statute, has become practically a dead letter. They are debarred from filling even moderately high positions, either in the army, or in any public or private capacity. And attempts are made to crowd them out of business also. "No dealing with Jews!"

Attacks in Parliaments, in assemblies, in the press, in the pulpit, in the streets, on journeys—for example, their exclusion from certain hotels—even in places of recreation, become daily more numerous, the forms of persecution varying according to the countries in which they occur. In Russia, impositions are levied on Jewish villages; in Roumania, a few human beings are put to death; in Germany, they get a good beating when the occasion serves; in Austria, Anti-Semites exercise terrorism over all public life; in Paris, they are shut out of the so-called best social circles and excluded from clubs. Shades of Anti-Jewish feeling are innumerable. But this is not to be an attempt to make out a doleful category of Jewish hardships; it is futile to linger over details, however painful they may be.

I do not intend to awaken sympathetic emotions on our behalf. That would be a foolish, futile, and undignified proceeding. I shall content myself with putting the following questions to the Jews: Is it true that, in countries where we live in perceptible numbers, the position of Jewish lawyers, doctors, men of science, teachers, and officials of all descriptions, becomes daily more intolerable? True, that the Jewish middle classes are seriously threatened? True, that the passions of the mob are incited against our wealthy representatives? True, that our poor endure greater sufferings than any other proletariat?

THE JEWISH STATE

I think that this external pressure makes itself felt everywhere. In our upper classes it causes unpleasantness, in our middle classes continual and grave anxieties, in our lower classes absolute despair.

Everything tends, in fact, to one and the same conclusion, which is clearly enunciated in that classic Berlin phrase: "Juden raus!" (Out with the Jews!)

I shall now put the Jewish Question in the curtest possible form: Are we to "get out" now? And if so, to what place?

Or, may we yet remain? And If so, how long?

Let us first settle the point of staying where we are. Can we hope for better days, can we possess our souls in patience, can we wait in pious resignation till the princes and peoples of this earth are more mercifully disposed towards us? I say that we cannot hope for a change in the current of feeling. And why not? Were we as near to the hearts of princes as are their other subjects, even so they could not protect us. They would only feed popular hatred of Jews by showing us too much favor. By "too much," I really mean less than is claimed as a right by every ordinary citizen, and by every tribe.

Every nation in whose midst Jews live is, either covertly or openly, Anti-Semitic.

The common people have not, and indeed cannot have, any historic comprehension. They do not know that the sins of the Middle Ages are now being visited on the nations of Europe. We are what the Ghetto made us. We have doubtless attained pre-eminence in finance, because mediaeval conditions drove us to it. The same process is now being repeated. Modern conditions force us again into finance, now the stock-exchange, by keeping us out of all other branches of industry. Being on the stock-exchange, we are therefore again considered contemptible. At the same time we continue to produce an abundance of mediocre intellects which finds no outlet, and this endangers our social position as much as does our increasing wealth. Educated Jews without means are now fast becoming Socialists. Hence we are certain to suffer very severely in the struggle between classes, because we stand in the most exposed position in the camps of both Socialists and capitalists.

The Jewish Question

PREVIOUS ATTEMPTS AT A SOLUTION

The artificial means heretofore employed to overcome the troubles of Jews have been either too petty—such as attempts at colonization, or mistaken in principle—such as attempts to convert the Jews into peasants in their present homes.

What is the result of transporting a few thousand Jews to another country? Either they come to grief at once, or prosper, and then their prosperity creates Anti-Semitism. We have already discussed these attempts to divert poor Jews to fresh districts. This diversion is clearly inadequate and futile, if it does not actually defeat its own ends; for it merely protracts and postpones a solution, and perhaps even aggravates difficulties.

Whoever were to attempt a conversion of the Jews into a husbandman would be making an extraordinary mistake. For a peasant is a historical category, as is proved by his costume, which in some countries he has worn for centuries; and by his tools, which are identical with those used by his earliest forefathers. His plough is unchanged; he carries the seed in his apron; mows with the historical scythe, and threshes with the time-honored flail. But we know that all this can be done by machinery. The agrarian question is only a question of machinery. America must conquer Europe, in the same way as large landed possessions absorb small ones.

The peasant is consequently a type which is in course of extinction. Whenever he is artificially preserved, it is done on account of the political interests which he is intended to serve. It is absurd, and indeed impossible, to make modern peasants on the old pattern. No one is wealthy or powerful enough to make civilization take a single retrograde step. The mere preservation of obsolete institutions is a task severe enough to require the enforcement of all the despotic measures of an autocratically governed State.

Are we therefore to credit Jews, who are intelligent, with a desire to become peasants of the old type? One might just as well say to them: "Here is a cross-bow; now go to war?" What? with a cross-bow, while the others have rifles and Maxim guns? Under these circumstances the Jews are perfectly justified in refusing to stir when people try to agrarianize them. A cross-bow is a beautiful weapon, it inspires me with mournful feelings when I have time to give way. But it belongs rightly in a museum.

Now, there certainly are districts where desperate Jews go out, or at any rate are willing to go out, and till the soil. And a little observation shows that these districts—such as portions of Hessen in Germany, and some provinces in Russia—these very districts are the principal seats of Anti-Semitism.

For the world's reformers, who send the Jews to the plough, forget a very important person, who has a decided objection to seeing them there. This person is the agriculturist. And the agriculturist is also perfectly justified in his objections. For the tax on land, the risks attached to crops, the pressure of large proprietors who cheapen labor, and American competition in particular, combine to make his life hard enough. The duties on corn cannot go on increasing indefinitely. Nor can the manufacturer be allowed to starve; his political influence is, in fact, in the ascendant, and he must therefore be treated with additional consideration.

All these difficulties are well known, therefore I only referred to them cursorily. I merely wanted to indicate clearly how futile had been past attempts—most of them well intentioned—to solve the Jewish Question. Neither a diversion of the stream, nor an artificial depression of the intellectual level of our proletariat, will overcome the difficulty. The supposed infallible expedient of assimilation has already been dealt with.

We cannot get the better of Anti-Semitism by any of these methods. It cannot die out so long as its causes are not removed. Are they removable?

CAUSES OF ANTI-SEMITISM.

We shall not again touch on those causes which are a result of temperament, prejudice and limited views, but shall here restrict ourselves to political and economic causes alone. Modern Anti-Semitism is not to be confounded with the religious persecution of the Jews of former times. It does occasionally take a somewhat religious bias, but the main current of the aggressive movement

The Jewish Question

has now changed. In the principal countries where Anti-Semitism prevails, it does so as a result of the emancipation of the Jews. When civilized nations awoke to the inhumanity of exclusive legislation and enfranchised us, our enfranchisement came too late. It was no longer possible legally to remove our disabilities in our old homes. For we had, curiously enough, developed while in the Ghetto into a bourgeois people, and we stepped out of it only to enter into fierce competition with the middle classes. Hence, our emancipation set us suddenly within this middle-class circle, where we have a double pressure to sustain, from within and from without. The Christian bourgeoisie would not be unwilling to cast us as a sacrifice to Socialism, though that would not greatly improve matters. At the same time, the equal rights of Jews before the law cannot be withdrawn where they have once been conceded. Not only because their withdrawal would be opposed to the spirit of our age, but also because it would immediately drive all Jews, rich and poor alike, into the ranks of the revolutionary army.

Nothing effectual can really be done to our injury. In old days our jewels were seized. How is our movable property to be got hold of now? It is comprised in printed papers which are scattered over the world, locked up maybe in the coffers of Christians. It is of course possible to get at shares and debentures in railways, banks and industrial concerns of all descriptions, by taxation, and where the progressive income-tax is in force, all our realized property can eventually be laid hold of. But all these efforts cannot be directed against Jews alone, and where they have nevertheless been made, severe economic crises with far-reaching effects have been their immediate consequence. The very, impossibility of getting at the Jews nourishes and embitters hatred of them. Anti-Semitism increases day by day and hour by hour among the nations; indeed, it is bound to increase, because the causes of its growth continue to exist, and cannot be removed. Its remote cause is our loss of the power of assimilation during the Middle Ages; its immediate cause is our excessive production of mediocre intellects, who cannot find an outlet downwards or upwards—that is to say, no wholesome outlet in either direction. When we sink, we become a revolutionary proletariat, the subordinate officers of the revolutionary party; when we rise, there rises also our terrible power of the purse.

EFFECTS OF ANTI-SEMITISM.

The oppression we endure does not improve us, for we are not a whit better than ordinary people. It is true that we do not love our enemies; but he alone who can conquer himself dare reproach us with that fault. Oppression naturally creates hostility against oppressors, and our hostility aggravates the pressure. It is impossible to escape from this eternal round.

"No!" some soft-hearted visionaries will say; "no, it is possible! Possible by means of the ultimate perfection of humanity."

Is it worth while pointing out the sentimental folly of this view? He who would found his hope for improved conditions on the ultimate perfection of humanity, would indeed be painting a Utopia!

I referred previously to our "assimilation"; I do not for a moment wish to imply that I desire such an end. Our national character is too historically famous, and, spite of every degradation, too fine, to make its annihilation desirable. We might perhaps be able to merge ourselves entirely into surrounding races, if these were to leave us in peace for a space of two generations. But they will not leave us in peace. For a little period they manage to tolerate us, and then their hostility breaks out again and again. The world is provoked by our prosperity, because it has for many centuries been accustomed to consider us as the most contemptible among the poverty-stricken. It forgets, in its ignorance and narrowness of heart, that prosperity weakens our Judaism and extinguishes our peculiarities. It is only pressure that forces us back to the parent stem; it is only hatred encompassing us that makes us strangers once more.

Thus, whether we like it or not, we are now, and shall henceforth remain, a historic group with unmistakable characteristics common to us all.

We are one people—our enemies have made us one in our despite, as repeatedly happens in history. Distress binds us together, and, thus united, we suddenly discover our strength. Yes, we are strong enough to form a State, and a model State. We possess all human and material resources necessary for the purpose.

The Jewish Question

This is the strictly appropriate place for an account of what has been somewhat rudely termed our human material. But it would not be appreciated till the broad lines of the plan, on which everything depends, had first been marked out.

THE PLAN.

The whole plan is in its essence perfectly simple, as it must necessarily be if it is to come within the comprehension of all.

Let the sovereignty be granted us over a portion of the globe large enough to satisfy the reasonable requirements of a nation; the rest we shall manage for ourselves.

The creation of a new State is neither ridiculous nor impossible. We have in our day witnessed the process in connection with nations which were not in the bulk of the middle class, but poorer, less educated, and consequently weaker than ourselves. The Governments of all countries scourged by Anti-Semitism will serve their own interests in assisting us to obtain the sovereignty we want.

The plan, simple in design, but complicated in execution, will he carried out by two mediums: the Society of Jews and the Jewish Company.[*]

The Society of Jews will do the preparatory work in the domains of science and politics, which the Jewish Company will afterwards practically apply.

The Jewish Company will see to the realization of the business interests of departing Jews, and will organize commerce and trade in the new country.

We must not imagine the departure of the Jews to be a sudden one. It will be gradual, continuous, and will cover many decades. The poorest will go first to cultivate the soil. In accordance with a preconcerted plan, they will construct roads, bridges, railways, and telegraphs; regulate rivers, and build their own habitations; their labor will create trade, trade will create markets, and markets will attract new settlers; for every man will go voluntarily,

---

[*] These became subsequently the Zionist movement and the Jewish Colonial Trust, Ltd., respectively.

THE JEWISH STATE

at his own expense and his own risk. The labor expended on the land will enhance its value, and the Jews will soon perceive that a new and permanent sphere of operation is opening here for that spirit of enterprise which has heretofore met only with hatred and obloquy.

If we wish to found a State today, we shall not do it in the way which would have been the only possible one a thousand years ago. It is foolish to revert to old stages of civilization, as many Zionists would like to do. Supposing, for example, we were obliged to clear a country of wild beasts, we should not set about the business in the fashion of Europeans of the fifth century. We should not take spear and lance and go out singly in pursuit of bears; we should organize a large and active hunting party, drive the animals together, and throw a melinite bomb into their midst.

If we wish to conduct building operations, we shall not plant a mass of stakes and piles on the shore of a lake, but we shall build as men build now. Indeed, we shall build in a bolder and more stately style than was ever adopted before, for we now possess means which men never yet possessed.

The emigrants standing lowest in the economic scale will be slowly followed by those of a higher grade. Those who at this moment are living in despair will go first. They will be led by the mediocre intellects which we produce so superabundantly, and which are persecuted everywhere.

This pamphlet will open a general discussion on the Jewish Question, avoiding, if possible, the creation of an opposition party. Such a result would ruin the cause from the outset, and dissentients must remember that allegiance or opposition are entirely voluntary. Who will not come with us, may remain.

Let all who are willing to join us, fall in behind our banner and fight for our cause with voice and pen and deed.

Those Jews who fall in with our idea of a State will attach themselves to the Society, which will thereby be authorized to confer and treat with Governments in the name of our people. The Society will thus be acknowledged in its relations with Governments as a State-creating power. This acknowledgment will practically create the State.

The Jewish Question

Should the Powers declare themselves willing to admit our sovereignty over a neutral piece of land, then the Society will enter into negotiations for the possession of this land. Here two territories come under consideration, Palestine and Argentina. In both countries important experiments in colonization have been made, though on the mistaken principle of a gradual infiltration of Jews. An infiltration is bound to end in disaster. It continues till the inevitable moment when the native population feels itself threatened, and forces the Government to stop the further influx of Jews. Immigration is consequently futile unless based on an assured supremacy.

The Society of Jews will treat with the present masters of the land, putting itself under the protectorate of the European Powers, if they prove friendly to the plan. We could offer the present possessors of the land enormous advantages; take upon ourselves part of the public debt, build new roads for traffic, which our presence in the country would render necessary, etc. The creation of our State would be beneficial to adjacent countries, because the cultivation of a strip of land increases the value of its surrounding districts in innumerable ways.

PALESTINE OR ARGENTINA?

Shall we choose Palestine or Argentina?* We shall take what is given us, and what is selected by Jewish public opinion. The Society will settle both these points.

Argentina is one of the most fertile countries in the world, extends over a vast area, has a sparse population and a mild climate. The Argentine Republic would derive considerable profit from the cession of a portion of its territory to us. The present infiltration of Jews has certainly produced some friction, and it would be necessary to enlighten the Republic on the intrinsic difference of our new movement.

Palestine is our ever-memorable historic home. The very name of Palestine would attract our people with a force of marvellous potency. Supposing His Majesty the Sultan were to

---

* See editor's preface for the determining of this issue.

give us Palestine, we could in return pledge ourselves to regulate the whole finances of Turkey. We should there form a portion of the rampart of Europe against Asia, an outpost of civilization as opposed to barbarism. The sanctuaries of Christendom would be safeguarded by assigning to them an extra-territorial status, such as is well known to the law of nations. We should form a guard of honor about these sanctuaries, answering for the fulfilment of this duty with our existence. This guard of honor would be the great symbol of the solution of the Jewish Question after eighteen centuries of Jewish suffering.

DEMAND, MEDIUM, TRADE.

I said in the last chapter but one, "the Jewish Company will organize trade and commerce in the new country." I shall here insert a few remarks on that point.

A scheme such as mine is gravely imperilled by the antagonistic attitude of "experts." Now experts are often nothing more than men sunk into the groove of daily routine, whence they have an extraordinarily limited view. At the same time, their adverse opinion carries great weight, and can do considerable harm to a new project, at any rate till this new thing is sufficiently strong to throw "experts" and their stupid notions to the winds.

In the earliest period of European railway construction some "experts" were of opinion that it was foolish to build certain lines, "because there were not even sufficient passengers to fill the mail-coaches." They did not realize the truth which now seems obvious to us—that travelers do not produce railways, but, conversely, railways produce travelers, the latent demand being, of course, taken for granted.

The impossibility of comprehending how trade and commerce are to be created in a new country which has yet to be acquired and cultivated may be classed with those doubts of "experts" concerning the need for railways. An "expert" would express himself somewhat in this fashion:

"Granted that the present situation of the Jews is in many places unendurable, and aggravated day by day; granted that there exists a desire to emigrate; granted even that the Jews do emigrate

The Jewish Question

to the new country; how will they earn their living there, and what will they earn? What are they to live on when there? Commerce cannot be artificially organized in a day."

To this I should reply: We have not the slightest intention of organizing trade artificially, and we should certainly not attempt to do it in a day. But, though the organization of it may be impossible, the promotion of it is not. And how is commerce to be encouraged? Through the medium of a demand. The demand recognized, the medium created, commerce will establish itself.

If there is a real and earnest demand among Jews for an improvement of their status; if the medium to be created—the Jewish Company—is sufficiently powerful, then commerce will extend itself copiously in the new country. This is, of course, an assumption, in the same way as the development of railway traffic was an assumption in the thirties. Railroads were built all the same, for men's ideas fortunately carried them beyond the doubts of "experts" and their mail-coaches.

OUTLINES.

The Jewish Company is partly modelled on the lines of a great trading association. It might be called a Jewish Chartered Company, though it cannot exercise sovereign power, and has duties other than the establishment of colonial commerce.

The Jewish Company will be founded as a joint-stock company subject to English jurisdiction, framed according to English laws, and under the protection of England. Its principal centre will be London. I cannot tell yet how large the Company's capital should be; I shall leave that calculation to our numerous financiers. But to avoid ambiguity, I shall put it at a thousand million marks (about £50,000,000); it may be either more or less than that sum. The form of subscription, which will be further elucidated, will determine what fraction of the whole amount must be paid in at once.

The Jewish Company is an organization with a transitional character. It is strictly a business undertaking, and must be carefully distinguished from the Society of Jews.

THE JEWISH STATE

The Jewish Company will first of all see to the realization of all vested interests left by departing Jews. The method adopted will prevent the occurrence of crises, secure every man's property, and facilitate that inner migration of Christian citizens which has already been indicated.

NON-TRANSFERABLE GOODS.

The non-transferable goods which come under consideration are house property, land, and local business connections. The Jewish Company will at first take upon itself no more than the necessary negotiations for effecting the sale of these goods. These Jewish sales will not immediately produce any serious fall in prices. The Company's branch establishments in various towns will become the central offices for the sale of Jewish estates, and will charge only so much commission on transactions as will insure their financial stability.

Now, the development of this movement may cause a considerable fall in the prices of landed property, and may eventually make it impossible to find a market for it. At this juncture the Company will enter upon another branch of its functions. It will take over the management of abandoned estates till such time as it can dispose of them to greatest advantage. It will rent houses, let out land on lease, and instal business managers—these, on account of the required supervision, being, if possible, tenants also. The Company will endeavor everywhere to facilitate the acquisition of land by its tenants, who are Christians. It will, indeed, gradually replace its own officials in the European branches by Christian substitutes; lawyers, etc; and these are not by any means to become servants of the Jews; they are intended to be free controlling bodies to the Christian population, so that everything may be carried through in equity, fairness and justice, and without imperilling the internal welfare of the people.

At the same time the Company will buy estates, or, rather, exchange them. For a house it will offer a house in the new country, and for land, land in the new country; everything being, if possible, transferred to new soil in the same state as it was in the old. And this transfer will be a great and recognized source of profit to the Company. "Over there" the houses offered in exchange will be newer, more beautiful, and more comfortably fitted, and the landed estates of greater value than those abandoned; but they will cost the Company comparatively little, because it will have bought the ground at a very cheap rate.

PURCHASE OF LAND.

The land which the Society of Jews will have secured by international law must, of course, be privately acquired.

Provisions made by individuals for their own settlement do not come within the province of this general account. But the Company requires large strips of territory for its own needs and ours, and these it must secure by private purchase. It will negotiate principally for the acquisition of fiscal domains, with the great object of taking possession of this land "over there" without paying a price too high, in the same way as it sells here without accepting one too low. A forcing of prices will be impossible, because the value of the land will be created by the Company through its organization of settlements, in conjunction with the supervising Society of Jews. The latter will see to it that the enterprise does not become a Panama, but a Suez.

The Company will sell building sites at cheap rates to its officials, and will allow them to mortgage these for the building of their habitations, deducting the amount due from their salaries, or putting it down to their account as increased emolument. This will, in addition to the honors they expect, form a kind of recompense for their services.

All the immense profits of this speculation in land will go to the Company, which is bound to receive this indefinite premium in return for having borne the risk of the undertaking. When the undertaking involves any risk, the profits must be freely accorded to those who have borne it. But under no other circumstances will profits be permitted. In the co-relation of risk and profit is comprehended financial justice.

BUILDINGS.

The Company will thus barter houses and estates. It must be plain to any one who has observed the rise in the value of land through its cultivation, that the Company will gain enormously on its landed property. This can best be seen in enclosed pieces of land in town and country. Areas not built over increase in value through surrounding cultivation. The men who carried out the extension of Paris made a successful speculation in land which was ingenious in its simplicity; instead of erecting new buildings in the immediate vicinity of the last houses of the town, they bought up adjacent strips of land and began to build on the outskirts of these. This inverse order of construction raised the value of building sites with extraordinary rapidity. After having completed the outer ring, they built in the middle of the town on these highly valuable sites, instead of continually erecting houses at the extremity.

Will the Company do its own building, or commission independent architects? It can, and will, do both. It has, as will be shown shortly, an immense reserve of working power, which will not be sweated by the Company, but, transported into brighter and happier conditions of life, will work at a cheap rate. Our geologists will have looked to the provision of building materials when they selected the sites of the towns.

What is to be the principle of construction?

WORKMEN'S DWELLINGS.

The workmen's dwellings (which include the dwellings of all operatives) will be erected at the Company's own risk and expense. They will resemble neither those melancholy workmen's barracks of European towns, nor those miserable rows of cabins which surround factories; they will certainly present a uniform appearance, because the Company must build cheaply where it provides the building materials to a great extent; but the detached houses in little gardens will be united into attractive groups in each locality. The natural conformation of the land will rouse the ingenuity of our young architects, whose ideas have not yet been

The Jewish Question

cramped by routine; and even if the people do not grasp the whole import of the plan, they will at any rate feel at ease in their loose clusters. The Temple will be visible from long distances, for our faith it was that united us in the old days. There will be light, attractive, healthy schools for children, conducted on the most approved modern systems. There will be continuation-schools for workmen, which will educate them up to greater technical knowledge and enable them to become intimate with the working of machinery. There will be places of amusement, for the proper conduct of which the Society of Jews will be responsible.

We are, however, speaking merely of the buildings at present, not of what may take place inside them.

I said that the Company would build workmen's dwellings cheaply. And cheaply, not only because of the proximity of abundant building materials, not only because of the Company's proprietorship of the sites, but also because of the non-payment of workmen.

American farmers work on the system of mutual assistance in the construction of houses. This childishly amicable system, which is as clumsy as the block houses erected, allows of considerable amplifications.

UNSKILLED LABORERS.

Our unskilled laborers, who will come at first from the great reservoirs of Russia and Roumania, must, of course, render each other assistance in the construction of houses. They will be obliged to build with wood in the beginning, because iron will not be immediately available. Later on, the original, inadequate, makeshift buildings will be replaced by superior dwellings.

Our unskilled laborers will first mutually erect these shelters; and then they will earn their houses as permanent possessions by means of their work—not immediately, but after three years of good conduct. In this way we shall secure energetic and able men, and these men will be practically trained for life by three years of labor under good discipline.

I said before that the Company would not have to pay these unskilled laborers. What will they live on?

THE JEWISH STATE

On the whole, I am opposed to the Truck system, but it will have to be applied in the case of these first settlers. The Company provides for them in so many ways that it may take entire charge of their maintenance. In any case the Truck system will be enforced only during the first few years, and it will benefit the workmen by preventing their exploitation by small traders, landlords, etc. The Company will thus make it impossible from the outset for those of our people who are perforce hawkers and pedlars here to re-establish themselves in the same trades over there. And the Company will also keep back drunkards and dissolute men. Then there will be no payment of wages at all during the first period of settlement?

Wages will be paid for overtime.

THE SEVEN-HOURS DAY.

The seven-hours day is the regular working day.

This does not imply that wood-cutting, digging, stone-breaking, and a hundred other daily tasks should only be performed during seven hours. Indeed not. There will be fourteen hours of labor, work being done in shifts of three and a half hours. The organization of all this will be military in character; there will be commands, promotions and pensions, the means by which these pensions are raised being explained further on.

A sound man can do an excellent piece of work in three hours and a half. After an interval of the same length of time—which he will devote to rest, to his family, and to his education under guidance—he will be quite fresh for work again. Such labor can do wonders.

The seven-hours day thus implies fourteen hours of joint labor—more than that cannot be put into a day.

I am convinced that it is quite possible to introduce this seven-hours day with success. The attempts to do so in Belgium and England are well known. Some advanced political economists who have studied the subject declare that a five-hours day would actually suffice. The Society of Jews and the Jewish Company will, in any case, make new and extensive experiments which will benefit the other nations of the world; and if the seven-hours day proves itself practicable, it will be introduced in our future State as the legal and regular working day.

Meantime the Company will always allow its employés the seven-hours day; and it will always be in a position to do so.

The seven-hours day will be the call of assembly to our people in every part of the world. All must come voluntarily, for ours must indeed be the Promised Land. . . .

Whoever works longer than seven hours receives his additional pay for overtime in cash. Seeing that all his needs are supplied, and that those members of his family who are unable to work are provided for by transplanted and centralized philanthropic institutions, he can put a little money by. Thrift, which is already a characteristic of our people, should be greatly encouraged, because it will, in the first place, facilitate the rise of individuals to higher grades; and secondly, the money saved will provide an immense reserve fund for future loans. Overtime will only be permitted on a doctor's certificate, and must not exceed three hours. For our men will crowd to work in the new country, and the world will see then what stuff for work is in us.

I shall not describe the mode of carrying out the Truck system, nor, in fact, the innumerable details of any process, for fear of confusing my readers. Women will not be allowed to perform any arduous labor, nor to work overtime.

Pregnant women will be relieved of all work, and will be supplied with nourishing food by the Truck. We want our future generations to be strong men and women.

We shall educate children as we wish from the commencement; but this I shall not elaborate either.

My remarks on workmen's dwellings, and on unskilled laborers and their mode of life, are no more Utopian than the rest of my scheme. Everything I have spoken of has already been put into practice on a small and insignificant scale. The "Assistance par le Travail," or "labor-test," which I studied in Paris, was of great service to me in the solution of the Jewish Question.

THE LABOR-TEST.

The labor-test which is now applied in Paris, in many other French towns, in England, in Switzerland, and in America, is a very small thing, but capable of the greatest expansion.

What is the principle of the labor-test.

The principle is: the furnishing of every necessitous man with easy, unskilled work, such as chopping wood, or cutting faggots used for lighting stoves in Paris households. This is a kind of prison-work *before* the crime, done without loss of character. It is meant to prevent men from taking to crime out of want, by providing them with work and testing their willingness to do it. Starvation must never be allowed to drive men to suicide; for such suicides are the deepest disgrace to a civilization which allows rich men to throw tit-bits to their dogs.

The labor-test thus provides every one with work. But the system has a great defect: there is not a sufficiently large demand for the productions of the unskilled workers employed, hence there is a loss to those who employ them; though it is true that the organization is philanthropic, and therefore prepared for loss. But here the benefaction lies only in the difference between the price paid for the work and its actual value. Instead of giving the beggar two sous, the institution supplies him with work on which it loses two sous. But at the same time it converts the good-for-nothing beggar into an honest bread-winner, who has earned perhaps 1 franc 50 centimes. 150 centimes for 10! That is to say, the receiver of a benefaction in which there is nothing humiliating has increased it fifteenfold! That is to say, fifteen thousand millions for one thousand millions!

The institution certainly loses 10 centimes. But the Jewish Company will not lose one thousand millions; it will draw enormous profits from this expenditure.

There is a moral side also. The small labor-tests which exist now preserve rectitude through industry till such time as the man who is out of work finds a post suitable to his capacities, either in his old calling or in a new one. He is allowed an hour or two daily for the purpose of looking for a place, in which task the institutions assist him.

The Jewish Question

The defect of these small organizations, so far, has been that they have been prohibited from entering into competition with timber merchants, etc. Timber merchants are electors; they would protest, and would be justified in protesting. Competition with State prison-labor has also been forbidden, for the State must have the monopoly of tending and exploiting its criminals.

In fact, there is very little room in an old-established society for the successful application of labor-tests.

But there is room in a new society!

For, above all, we require enormous numbers of unskilled laborers to do the first rough work of settlement, to lay down roads, plant trees, level the ground, lay down railroads and telegraph lines, etc. All this being, of course, carried out in accordance with a great and previously settled plan.

COMMERCE.

The labor carried to the new country will naturally create trade. The first markets will supply only the absolute necessaries of life: cattle, grain, working clothes, tools, arms, etc. These we shall be obliged at first to procure from neighboring States, or from Europe; but we shall make ourselves independent as soon as possible. The Jewish promoters will soon realize what prospects of business the new country offers.

The army of the Company's officials will gradually introduce more refined requirements of life. (Officials include officers of our defensive forces, who will always form about the tenth part of our male colonists. They will be sufficiently numerous to quell mutinies, for the majority of our colonists will be peaceably inclined.)

The refined requirements of life introduced by our more prosperous officials will create a correspondingly improved market, which will continue to better itself. The married man will send for wife and children, and the bachelor for parents and relatives, as soon as a new home is established "over there." The Jews who emigrate to the United States always proceed in this fashion. As soon as one of them has daily bread and a roof over his head, he sends for his people; for family ties are strong among us. The

Society of Jews and the Jewish Company will unite in caring for and strengthening the family, not only morally, but materially also. The officials will receive an increase of salary on marriage, and on the birth of children, for we need all who are there, and all who will follow.

OTHER CLASSES OF DWELLINGS.

I described before only workmen's dwellings built by themselves, and omitted all mention of other classes of dwellings; these I shall now touch upon. The Company's architects will build for the poorer class of citizens also, being paid in kind or cash; about a hundred different types of houses will be executed, and, of course, repeated. These beautiful types will form part of our propaganda. The soundness of their construction will be guaranteed by the Company, which will, indeed, gain nothing by selling them to settlers at a fixed sum. And where will these houses be situated? That will shortly be demonstrated in the description of local groups.

Seeing that the Company receives, as it were, ground-rent and not house-rent, it will desire as many architects as possible to build by private contract. This system will introduce luxury, which serves many purposes. Luxury encourages arts and industries, paving the way to a future subdivision of large properties.

Rich Jews who are now obliged carefully to secrete their valuables, and to hold their dreary banquets behind lowered curtains, will be able to enjoy their possessions in peace "over there." If they cooperate in carrying out this emigration scheme, their capital will be rehabilitated there, and will have served to promote an unexampled undertaking. If rich Jews begin to rebuild their mansions in the new settlement, where they are no longer surveyed with envious eyes, it will soon become fashionable to live over there in beautiful modern houses.

SOME FORMS OF REALIZING NON-TRANSFERABLE PROPERTY

The Jewish Company is the receiver and administrator of the

non-transferable goods of the Jews.

Its methods of procedure can be easily imagined in the case of houses and estates, but what methods will it adopt in the transfer of businesses?

Here numberless processes may be found practicable, which cannot all be enlarged on in this outline. But none of them will present any great difficulties, for in each case the emigrating business proprietor will settle with the Company's officers in his district on the most advantageous form of liquidation.

This will most easily be arranged in the case of small employers, in whose trades the personal activity of the proprietor is of chief importance, while goods and organization are a secondary consideration. The Company will provide a certain field of operation for the emigrant's personal activity, and will substitute a piece of ground, with loan of machinery, for his goods. Jews are known to adapt themselves with remarkable ease to any form of earning a livelihood, and they will quickly learn to carry on a new industry. In this way a number of small traders will become small landholders. The Company will, in fact, be prepared to sustain what appears to be a loss in taking over the non-transferable property of the poorest emigrants; for it will thereby induce the free cultivation of tracts of land, which raises the value of adjacent tracts.

In a larger business, where goods and organization equal, or even exceed, in importance, the personal activity of the manager, whose larger connection is also non-transferable, various forms of liquidation are possible. Here comes an opportunity for that inner migration of Christian citizens into positions evacuated by Jews. The departing Jew will not lose his personal business credit, but will carry it with him. The Jewish Company will open a current bank account for him. And he can sell the goodwill of his original business, or hand it over to the control of managers under supervision of the Company's officials. The managers may rent the business or buy it, paying for it by instalments. But the Company acts temporarily as trustee for the emigrants, in superintending, through its officers and lawyers, the administration of their affairs, and seeing to the correct entry of all accounts.

If a Jew cannot sell his business, will not entrust it to a proxy, and does not wish to give up its personal management, he may stay where he is. The Jews who stay will be none the worse off, for they will be relieved of the competition of those who leave, and will no longer hear the Anti-Semitic cry "No dealing with Jews!"

If the emigrating business proprietor wishes to carry on his old business in the new country, he can make his arrangements for it from the very commencement. An example will best illustrate my meaning. The firm X. carries on a large business in fancy goods. The head of the firm wishes to emigrate. He begins by setting up a branch establishment in his future place of residence, and sending out his surplus stock. The first poor settlers will be his first customers; these will be followed by emigrants of a higher class, who require superior goods. X. then sends out newer goods, and eventually despatches his newest. The branch establishment begins to pay while the principal one is still in existence, so that X. ends by having two paying business houses. He sells his original business to a Christian, and goes off to manage the new one.

Another and greater example: Y. & Son are large coal traders, with mines and factories of their own. How is so huge and complex a property to be realized? The mines and everything connected with them might, in the first place, be bought up by the State in which they are situated. In the second place, the Jewish Company might take them over, paying for them partly in land, partly in cash. A third method might be the conversion of Y. & Son into a limited company. A fourth, the continued working of the business under the original proprietors, who would return at intervals to inspect their property, as foreigners, and as such, under the protection of law in every civilized State. All these suggestions are carried out daily. A fifth method, and one which might be particularly profitable, I shall merely indicate, because there are at present few and feeble extant examples of its working, however ready the modern consciousness may be to adopt them. Y. & Son might sell their undertaking to the collective body of their employés, who would form a cooperative society, and might perhaps pay the requisite sum by means of a Government loan, on which there would not be heavy interest to pay.

The Jewish Question

The employés would then gradually pay off the loan which either the Government or the Jewish Company, or even Y. & Son, would have advanced to them.

The Jewish Company will be prepared to conduct the transfer of the smallest affairs equally with the largest. While Jewish emigration slowly proceeds, the Company remains its great controlling body, which organizes the departure, takes charge of deserted possessions, guarantees the proper conduct of the movement with its own visible and palpable property, and provides permanent security for those who have already settled.

SECURITIES OF THE COMPANY.

What securities will the Company offer that the abandonment of countries will not cause their impoverishment and produce economic crises?

I have already mentioned that honest Anti-Semites will combine with our officials in controlling the transfer of our estates.

But the State revenues might suffer by the loss of a body of taxpayers, who, though little appreciated as citizens, are highly valued in finance. The State should therefore receive compensation for this loss. This we offer indirectly by leaving in the country business which we have built up by means of Jewish shrewdness and Jewish industry, by letting our Christian fellow-citizens move into our evacuated positions, and by thus facilitating the rise of numbers of people to greater prosperity in a manner so peaceable as has never been known before. The French Revolution had a similar result, on a small scale, brought about by bloodshed on the guillotine, in every province of France, and on the battlefields of Europe. Moreover, inherited and acquired rights were destroyed, and cunning buyers only enriched themselves by the purchase of State properties.

The Jewish Company will offer to the States that fall under its sphere of work, direct as well as indirect advantages. It will give Governments the first offer of abandoned Jewish property, and allow buyers most favorable conditions. Governments, again, will be able to make use of this extensive appropriation of land for the purpose of social experiments and improvements.

THE JEWISH STATE

The Jewish Company will give every assistance to Governments and Parliaments in their efforts to control and guide the inner migration of Christian citizens.

The Jewish Company will also pay heavy duties. Its central office will be in London, so as to be under the protection of a Power which is not at present Anti-Semitic. But the Company requires to be officially and publicly supported, and must therefore be in a position to pay taxes. To this end, it will establish taxable branch offices everywhere. Further, it will pay double duties on the two-fold transfer of goods which it effects. Even in transactions where the Company is really nothing more than a business agency, it will temporarily appear as a purchaser, and will be set down as the momentary possessor in the register of landed property.

These are, of course, purely calculable matters.

Every place will raise and discuss the question, how far the Company can go without running any risks of failure. And the Company itself will confer freely with Finance Ministers on the various points at issue. Ministers will recognize the conciliatory spirit of our enterprise, and will consequently offer every facility in their power for the successful achievement of the great undertaking.

Further and direct profit will accrue to Governments from the transport of passengers and goods, and where railways are State property the returns will be immediately recognizable. Where they are held by companies, the Jewish Company will make favorable terms for transport, in the same way as does every transmitter of goods on a large scale. Freight and carriage must be made as cheap as possible for our people, because every traveler will pay his own expenses. The middle classes will travel with Cooks tickets, the poorer classes in emigrant trains. The Company might make a good deal by reductions on passengers and goods; but here, as elsewhere, it must adhere to its principle of not trying to raise its receipts to a greater sum than will cover its working expenses.

In many places Jews have control of the transport; and the transport industries will be the first needed by the Company, and the first to be bought up by it. The original owners of these

The Jewish Question

industries will either enter the Company's service, or establish themselves independently "over there." The new arrivals will certainly require their assistance, and theirs being a paying profession, which they may and indeed must exercise there to earn a living, numbers of these enterprising spirits will depart. It is unnecessary to describe all the business details of this monster expedition. They must be judiciously evolved out of the original plan by many able and intelligent men.

SOME OF THE COMPANY'S FUNCTIONS.

One department of work will create another. For example: the Company will introduce manufactures of goods into the settlements which will, of course, be extremely primitive at their inception. Outer garments, under-linen, and shoes will first of all be manufactured for our own poor emigrants, who will be provided with new suits of clothing at the various European emigration centres. They will not receive these clothes as alms, which might hurt their pride, but in exchange for old garments; any loss the Company sustains by this transaction being booked as a business loss. Those who are absolutely without means will pay off their debt to the Company by working overtime at a fair rate of wages.

Existing emigration societies will be able to give valuable assistance here, for they will do for the Company's colonists what they did before for departing Jews; a good system of cooperation being easily organized by the authorities.

The new clothing even of the poor settlers will have a symbolic meaning. "You are now entering on a new life." The Society of Jews will impress on them the solemnity and gravity of their undertaking by instituting the recital of prayers, popular lectures, instruction on the object of the expedition, directions on the hygienic construction of their new places of residence, and encouragement to work, before the departure and during the journey. On their arrival the emigrants will be welcomed by our chief officials with due solemnity, but without foolish exultation, for the Promised Land will not yet have been conquered; they will

THE JEWISH STATE

only feel that, poor as they are, they are on land of their own at last.

The clothing industries of the Company will, of course, not produce their goods without distinct organization. The Society of Jews will obtain from the local groups an exact estimate of the number, requirements, and date of arrival of the settlers, and will communicate all information in good time to the Jewish Company. In this way it will be possible to provide for them with every precaution.

PROMOTION OF INDUSTRIES.

The duties of the Jewish Company and the Society of Jews cannot be kept strictly apart in this outline. These two great bodies will indeed work in unison, the Company depending on the moral direction and support of the Society, the Society again acting only with the material assistance of the Company. For example, in the management of the clothing industry, the quantity produced will at first be kept down so as to preserve an equilibrium between supply and demand; and wherever the Company undertakes the organization of new industries the same precautions will be exercised.

But individual enterprise must never be checked by our superior force. We shall only work collectively when the immense difficulties of the task demand common action; we shall, wherever possible, scrupulously respect the rights of the individual. Private property, which is the economic basis of independence, will also be encouraged to develop freely. Our unskilled laborers even will work their way up to private proprietorship.

The spirit of enterprise must, indeed, he encouraged in every possible way. Organization of industries will be promoted by a judicious system of duties, by the employment of cheap raw material, and by the institution of a Board to collect and publish industrial statistics.

But this spirit of enterprise must he wisely encouraged, risky speculation being as far as possible avoided. Every newly established industry must be long previously advertised, so as to prevent promoters, who six months later might wish to start a similar business, from preparing for themselves a financial failure. If the Company carefully publishes the designs of every new scheme, a knowledge of existing industrial conditions will be obtained by every one.

Promoters will further be able to make use of centralized labor agencies, which will only receive a commission large enough to ensure their continuance. The promoter might, for example, telegraph for 500 unskilled laborers for three days, three weeks, or three months. The labor agency would then collect these 500 unskilled laborers from every possible source, and despatch them at once to carry out the agricultural or industrial undertaking. Gangs of workmen will thus he systematically drafted from place to place like a body of troops. These men will, of course, not be sweated, but will work only a seven-hours day; and, in spite of their change of locality, they will preserve their military organization, work out their term of service, and receive commands, promotions, and pensions. Independent promoters will, of course, be able to obtain their workmen from other sources, but they will not find it easy to do so. The Society will he able to prevent the introduction of the sweating system through non-Jewish workmen who would work overtime, by boycotting the employers of these, by controlling traffic, and by various other methods. The seven-hours day must therefore be adhered to, and we shall thus bring our people gradually, and without coercion, to adopt the normal seven-hours day.

SETTLEMENT OF SKILLED LABORERS.

What can be done for unskilled workers can obviously be more easily done for skilled laborers. These will work under similar regulations in the factories, and the central labor agency will provide them when required. Independent operatives and small employers, who must he carefully taught, on account of the rapid progress of scientific improvements, who must acquire technical knowledge even if no longer very young men, who must study the power of water, and appreciate the force of electricity—independent workers must also be discovered and supplied by the Society's agency. The local group might apply, for example, to the central office: "We want so many carpenters, locksmiths, glaziers, etc." The central office would publish this demand, and the proper men would apply there for the work. These would then travel with their families to the place where they were wanted, and would remain there without feeling the pressure of undue competition. A permanent and comfortable home would thus be provided for them.

METHOD OF RAISING CAPITAL.

The capital required for establishing the Company was previously put at what seemed an absurdly high figure. The amount actually necessary will be fixed by financiers, and will in any case be a very considerable sum. There are three ways of raising this sum, all of which the Society will take under consideration. This Society, the great "Gestor" of the Jews, will be formed by our best and most upright men, who must not derive any material advantage from their membership. Although the Society cannot at the outset possess any but moral authority, this authority will yet suffice to establish the credit of the Jewish Company in the nation's eyes. The Jewish Company will thus be unable to undertake any business enterprise which has not received the Society's sanction; it will also not be formed of any mere indiscriminate group of financiers. For the Society will weigh, select and decide, and will not give its approbation till it is sure of the existence of good securities for the conscientious carrying out of the scheme. It will not permit experiments with insufficient means, for this undertaking must succeed at the first attempt. Any initial failure would compromise the whole idea during many decades to come, or might even make its realization permanently impossible.

The three methods of raising capital are: (1) Through "la haute finance"; (2) Through small and private banks; (3) Through public subscription.*

The easiest, most rapid, and safest would be by "la haute finance." The required sum would then be raised in the shortest

---

* The third was adopted. The Jewish Colonial Trust was capitalized at £2,000,000, in £1 shares.

The Jewish Question

possible time by our great body of financiers, after they had discussed the advisability of the cause. The great advantage of this method would be that it would avoid the necessity of paying in the thousand millions (to keep to the original cipher) immediately in its entirety. A further advantage would be that the unlimited credit of these powerful financiers would be of considerable value to the Company in its transactions. Many latent political forces lie in our financial power, that power which our enemies assert to be actually and now as effective as we know it might be if we exercised it. Poor Jews feel only the hatred which this financial power provokes; its use in alleviating their lot as a body, they have not yet felt. The credit of our great Jewish financiers would have to be placed at the service of the National Idea. But should these gentlemen, who are naturally satisfied with their lot, decline to do anything for their co-religionists who are unjustly held responsible for the large possessions of certain individuals—should these great financiers refuse to cooperate—then the realization of this plan will afford an opportunity for drawing a clear line of distinction between them and the rest of Judaism.

The great financiers, moreover, will certainly not be asked to raise an amount so enormous out of pure philanthropy; that would be expecting too much. The promoters and stockholders of the Jewish Company are, on the contrary, intended to do a good piece of business, and they will be able to calculate beforehand what their chances of success are likely to be. For the Society of Jews will be in possession of all documents and references which may serve to define the prospects of the Jewish Company. The Society will also undertake the special duty of investigating with exactitude the extent of the new Jewish movement, so as to provide the Company promoters with thoroughly reliable information on the amount of support they may expect. The Society will also supply the Jewish Company with comprehensive modern Jewish statistics, thus doing the work of what is called in France a "société d'études," which undertakes all preliminary research previous to the financing of a great undertaking. Even so, the enterprise may not receive the valuable assistance of our money magnates. These might, perhaps, even try to oppose the Jewish movement by means of their secret servitors and agents. Such opposition we shall meet fairly and bravely.

THE JEWISH STATE

Supposing that these magnates are content simply to refuse their support of the scheme:

Is it, therefore, done with?

No.

For then the money will be raised in another way—by an appeal to moderately rich Jews. The smaller Jewish properties would have to be united in the name of the National Idea till they were gathered into a second and formidable financial force. But, unfortunately, this would require a great deal of financing at first—for the £50,000,000 would have to be subscribed in full before starting work; and, as this sum could only be raised very slowly, all sorts of banking business would have to be done and loans made during the first few years. It might even occur that, in the course of all these transactions, the ultimate object of them would be forgotten; Jews would create a new and large business, and forget all about emigration.

The notion of raising money in this way is not by any means impracticable. The experiment of collecting Christian money to form an opposing force to great financiers has already been tried; the experiment of opposing it with Jewish money has merely been thought of; it is quite feasible.

But these financial quarrels would bring about endless crises; the countries in which they occurred would suffer severely, and Anti-Semitism would become rampant everywhere.

This method is therefore not to be recommended. I have merely suggested it, because it comes up in the course of the logical development of the idea.

It is also doubtful whether smaller private banks would be willing to adopt it.

In any case, the refusal of moderately rich Jews would not even put an end to the scheme. A third method of carrying it out remains to be tried.

The Society of Jews, whose members are not business men, might try to found the Company on a national subscription.

The Company's capital might be raised without the assistance of a syndicate, by the direct imposition of a subscription on the public. Not only poor Jews, but also Christians who wanted to get rid of them, would subscribe their small quota to this fund. A new

The Jewish Question

and peculiar form of the *plebiscite* would thus be established, whereby each man who voted for this solution of the Jewish Question would express his favorable opinion by subscribing a stipulated amount. This stipulation would produce security. The funds subscribed would only be paid in if their sum total reached the required amount; if the tenders were not sufficiently numerous, they would be returned.

But should the sum total raised all over the world by a public tax reach the required amount, then each little subscription would be secured by the great numbers of other small subscriptions.

All this could, of course, not be done without the express and definite assistance of interested Governments.

LOCAL GROUPS

OUR TRANSMIGRATION.

PREVIOUS chapters explained only how the emigration scheme might be carried out without creating any economic disturbance. But so great a movement cannot take place without inevitably rousing many deep and powerful feelings. Old customs, old memories attach us to our homes. We have cradles, we have graves, and we alone know how Jewish hearts cling to the graves. Our cradles we shall carry with us—they hold our future, rosy and smiling. Our beloved graves we must, alas! abandon—and I think this abandonment will cost us covetous people more than any other sacrifice. But it must be so.

Economic distress, political pressure, and social obloquy have already driven us from our homes and from our graves. We Jews are even now perpetually shifting from place to place, a strong current actually carrying us westward over the sea to the United States, where our presence is not desired. And where will our presence be desired, so long as we are a homeless nation?

But we shall give a home to our people. And we shall give it, not by dragging them ruthlessly out of their sustaining soil, but rather by transplanting them carefully to a better ground. Though we are creating new political and economic relations, we shall preserve as sacred all that is dear to our people's hearts.

Here a few suggestions must suffice, as this part of my scheme will most probably be condemned as visionary. Yet even this is possible and real, though it now appears to be something vague and aimless. Organization will make of it something rational.

EMIGRATION IN GROUPS.

Our people may emigrate in groups of families and friends. But no man will be forced to join the particular group belonging to his former place of residence. Each will be able to journey in his chosen fashion as soon as he has settled his affairs. Seeing that each man will pay his own expenses by rail and boat, he will naturally travel by whatever class suits him best. Possibly there will even be no subdivision of classes on board train and boat, so as to avoid making the poor, who form the great majority of passengers, feel their position too keenly during their long journey. Though we are not exactly organizing a pleasure trip, it is as well to keep them in good humor on the way.

None will travel in penury; on the other hand all who desire to travel in luxurious ease will be able to follow their bent. Even under favorable circumstances, the movement may not touch certain classes of Jews for several years to come; the intervening period can therefore be employed in selecting the best modes of organizing the journeys. Those who are well off can travel in parties if they wish, taking their personal friends and connections with them. Jews, with the exception of the richest, have, after all, very little intercourse with Christians. In some countries their acquaintance with them is confined to a few spungers, borrowers, and dependents; of a better class of Christian they know nothing. The Ghetto subsists still, though its walls are broken down.

The middle classes will therefore make elaborate and careful preparations for departure. A group of travelers will be formed in each locality, large towns being divided into districts, with a group in each district, who will communicate by means of representatives elected for the purpose. This division into districts need not be strictly adhered to; it is merely intended to alleviate the discomfort and home-sickness of the poor during their journey outwards. If they so choose, they may either travel alone or attached to any local group they prefer. The conditions of travel—regulated according to classes—will apply to all alike. Any sufficiently numerous traveling party can charter a special train and special boat from the Company.

Local Groups

The Company's house agency will provide quarters for the poorest on their arrival. Later on, when more prosperous emigrants follow, their obvious need for lodgings on first landing will have been supplied by hotels built by private enterprise. Some of these more prosperous colonists will, indeed, have built their houses before becoming permanent settlers, so that they will merely move from an old home into a new one.

It would be an affront to our intelligence to point out everything that we might do. Every man who attaches himself to the National Idea will know how to spread it, and how to make it actual within his sphere of influence. We shall first of all ask for the cooperation of our ministers.

OUR MINISTERS.

Every group will have its minister, traveling with his congregation. Local groups will afterwards form voluntarily about their minister, and each locality will have its spiritual guide. Our ministers, on whom we especially call, will devote their energies to the service of our idea, and will inspire their congregations by preaching it from the pulpit. They will not need to address special meetings for the purpose; an appeal such as this may be uttered in the synagogue. And thus it must be done. For we feel our historic affinity only through the faith of our fathers; the very language of different nations has been impressed on us so deeply that it seems impossible to obliterate it.

The ministers will receive communications regularly from both Society and Company, and will announce and explain these to their congregations. Israel will pray for us and for itself.

RESPONSIBLE MEN OF THE LOCAL GROUPS.

The local groups will appoint small committees of responsible men under the minister's presidency, for discussion and settlement of local affairs.

Philanthropic institutions will be transferred by their local groups; each institution remaining "over there" the property of the same set of people for whom it was originally founded. I think the old buildings should not be sold, but rather devoted to the assistance of indigent Christians in the forsaken towns. The local group will receive compensation by obtaining free building sites and every facility for reconstruction in the new country.

This transfer of philanthropic institutions will give another of those opportunities which occur at different points of my scheme, for making an experiment in the service of humanity. Our present unsystematic private philanthropy does little good in proportion to the great expenditure it involves. But these institutions can and must form part of a system by which they will eventually supplement one another. In a new society these organizations can be evolved out of our modern consciousness, and may be based on all previous socio-political experiments. This matter is of great importance to us, on account of our large number of paupers. The weaker characters among us, discouraged by external pressure, spoilt by the soft-hearted charity of our rich men, easily sink, till they take to begging.

The Society, supported by the local groups, will give the greatest attention to popular education with regard to this particular. It will create a fruitful soil for many powers which now wither uselessly away. Whoever shows a genuine desire to work will be suitably employed. Beggars will not be endured. Whoever refused to do anything as a free man will be sent to the workhouse.

On the other hand, we shall not despatch the old to an infirmary. An infirmary is one of the cruelest charities which our stupid good-nature ever invented. There our old people die out of pure shame and mortification. There they are already buried. But we will leave to those even who stand on the lowest grade of intelligence the consoling illusion of their utility in the world. We will provide easy tasks for those who are incapable of physical labor; for we must allow for diminished vitality in the poor of an already enfeebled generation. But future generations shall be dealt with otherwise; they shall be brought up in liberty for a life of liberty.

We will seek to bestow the moral salvation of work on men of every age and of every class; and thus our people will find their strength again in the land of the seven-hours day.

Local Groups

PLANS OF THE TOWNS.

The local groups will delegate their representatives to select sites for towns. In the distribution of land, every precaution will be taken to effect a careful transfer with due consideration for acquired rights.

The local groups will have plans of the towns, so that our people may know beforehand where they are to go, in which towns and in which houses they are to live. Comprehensible drafts of the building plans previously referred to will be distributed among the local groups.

The principle of our administration will be strict centralization, of our local groups complete autonomy. In this way the transfer will be accomplished with the minimum of pain.

I do not imagine all this to be easier than it actually is; on the other hand, people must not imagine it to be more difficult than it is in reality.

THE DEPARTURE OF THE MIDDLE CLASSES.

The middle classes will involuntarily be drawn into the outgoing current, for their sons will be the Company's officials and employés over there." Lawyers, doctors, scientists of every description, young traders—in fact, all Jews who are in search of opportunities, who now escape from oppression in their native country to earn a living in foreign lands—will assemble on a soil so full of fair promise. The daughters of the middle classes will have married these ambitious men. One of them will send for his wife to come out to him, another for his parents, brothers and sisters. Members of a new civilization marry young. This can but promote general morality and ensure sturdiness in the scions of our race; and thus we shall have no delicate offspring of late marriages, children of fathers who spent their strength in the struggle for life.

Every middle-class emigrant will draw more of his kind after him.

The bravest will naturally get the best out of the new world.

But here we seem undoubtedly to have touched on the crucial difficulty of my plan.

THE JEWISH STATE

Even if we succeeded in opening a serious general discussion on the Jewish Question—

Even if this debate led us to a positive conclusion that the Jewish State were necessary to the world—

Even if the Powers assisted us in acquiring the sovereignty over a strip of territory—

How are we to transport masses of Jews without undue compulsion from their present homes to this new country?

Their emigration is surely voluntary?

THE PHENOMENON OF MULTITUDES.

Great exertions will not be necessary to spur on the movement. Anti-Semites provide the requisite impetus. They need only do what they did before, and then they will create a love of emigration where it did not previously exist, and strengthen it where it existed before. Jews who now remain in Anti-Semitic countries do so chiefly because, even those among them who are most ignorant of history, know that numerous changes of residence in bygone centuries never brought them any permanent good. Any land which welcomed the Jews today and offered them even fewer advantages than the future Jewish State would guarantee them, would immediately attract a great influx of our people. The poorest, who have nothing to lose, would drag themselves there. But I maintain, and every man may ask himself whether I am not right, that the pressure weighing on us rouses a desire to emigrate even among prosperous strata of society. Now our poorest strata alone would suffice to found a State; for these make the most vigorous conquerors, because a little despair is indispensable to the formation of a great undertaking.

But when our desperadoes increase the value of the land by their presence and by the labor they expend on it, they make it at the same time increasingly attractive as a place of settlement to people who are better off.

Higher and yet higher strata will feel tempted to go over. The expedition of the first and poorest settlers will be conducted by conjoint Company and Society, and will probably be additionally supported by existing emigration and Zionist societies.

Local Groups

How may a number of people be concentrated on a particular spot without being given express orders to go there? There are certain Jews, benefactors on a large scale, who try to alleviate the sufferings of their co-religionists by Zionist experiments. To them this problem also presented itself, and they thought to solve it by giving the emigrants money or means of employment. Thus the philanthropists said: "We pay these people to go there."

Such an experiment is utterly at fault, and all the money in the world will not achieve its purpose.

On the other hand, the Company will say: "We shall not pay them, we shall let them pay us. We shall merely offer them some inducement to go."

A fanciful illustration will make my meaning more explicit: One of these philanthropists (whom we will call "The Baron") and myself both wish to get a crowd of people on to the plain of Longchamps, near Paris, on a hot Sunday afternoon. The Baron, by promising them 10 francs each, will, for 200,000 francs, bring out 20,000 perspiring and miserable people, who will curse him for having given them so much annoyance. Whereas I will offer these 200,000 francs as a prize for the swiftest race-horse—and then I shall have to put up barriers to keep the people off Longchamps. They will pay to go in: 1 franc, 5 francs, 20 francs.

The consequence will be that I shall get half a million of people out there; the President of the Republic will drive *à la* Daumont; and the crowds will enjoy and amuse themselves. Most of them will think it an agreeable walk in the open air, spite of heat and dust; and I shall have made by my 200,000 francs about a million in entrance-money and taxes on gaming. I shall get the same people out there whenever I like; but the Baron will not—not on any account.

I will give a more serious illustration of the phenomenon of multitudes where they are earning a livelihood. Let any man attempt to cry through the streets of a town: "Whoever is willing to stand all day long through a winter's terrible cold, through a summer's tormenting heat, in an iron hall exposed on all sides, there to address every passer-by, and to offer him fancy wares, or fish, or fruit, will receive 2 florins, or 4 francs, or something similar."

How many people would go to the hall? How many days would they hold out when hunger drove them there? And if they held out, what energy would they display in trying to persuade passers-by to buy fish, fruit, and fancy wares?

We shall set about it in a different way. In places where trade is active, and these places we shall the more easily discover, since we ourselves form channels for trade to various localities; in these places we shall build large halls, and call them markets. These halls might be worse built and more unwholesome than those above mentioned, and yet people would stream towards them. But we shall use our best efforts, and we shall build them better, and make them more beautiful than the first. And the people, to whom we had promised nothing—because we cannot promise anything without deceiving them—these brave, keen business men will gaily create most active commercial intercourse. They will harangue the buyers unweariedly; they will stand on their feet, and scarcely think of fatigue. They will hurry off day after day, so as to be first on the spot; they will make agreements, promises, anything to continue bread-winning undisturbed. And if they find on Sabbath night that all their hard work has produced only 1 florin 50 kreuzer, or 3 francs, or something similar, they will yet look forward hopefully to the next day, which may, perhaps, bring them better luck.

We have given them hope.

Would any one ask whence the demand comes which creates the market? Is it really necessary to tell them again?

I pointed out before that the labor-test increased our gain fifteenfold. One million produced fifteen millions; and one thousand millions, fifteen thousand millions.

This may be the case on a small scale; is it so on a large one. Capital surely yields a return diminishing in inverse ratio to its own growth? Inactive capital yields this diminishing return, but active capital brings in a marvellously increasing return. Herein lies the social question.

Am I stating a fact? I call on the richest Jews as witnesses of my veracity. Why do these carry on so many different industries? Why do they send men to work underground and to raise coal amid terrible dangers for miserable pay? I cannot imagine this to

Local Groups

be pleasant, even for the owners of the mines. For I do not believe that capitalists are heartless, and I do not take up the attitude of believing it. My desire is not to accentuate, but to smooth differences.

Is it necessary to illustrate the phenomenon of multitudes, and their concentration on a particular spot, by references to pious pilgrimages?

I do not want to hurt any one's religious sensibility by words which might be wrongly interpreted.

I shall merely refer quite briefly to the Mahommedan pilgrimages to Mecca, the Catholic pilgrimages to Lourdes and to many other spots whence men return comforted by their faith, and to the holy Coat at Trier. Thus we shall also create a centre for the deep religious needs of our people. Our ministers will understand us first, and will be with us in this.

We shall let every man find salvation "over there" in his own particular way. Above and before all we shall make room for the immortal band of our Freethinkers, who are continually making new conquests for humanity.

No more force will be exercised on any one than is necessary for the preservation of the State and the upholding of its statutes; and the requisite force will not be arbitrarily defined by one or more shifting authorities; it will be fixed by iron laws.

Now if the illustrations I gave make people draw the inference that a multitude can be only temporarily attracted to centres of faith, of business, or of amusement, the reply to their objection is simple. Whereas one of these objects by itself would certainly only allure the masses, all these centres of attraction combined would be fully qualified permanently to hold and satisfy them. For all these centres together form a single, great, long-sought object, which our people has always longed to attain, for which it has kept itself alive, for which it has been kept alive by external pressure—a free home! When the movement commences, we shall draw some men after us and let others follow; others again will be swept into the current, and the last will be thrust after us.

These last hesitating colonists will be the worst off, both here and there.

But the first, who go over with faith, enthusiasm, and courage, will have the best of the bargain.

OUR INTRINSIC QUALITIES.

There are more mistaken notions abroad concerning Jews than concerning any other people. And we ourselves have become so depressed and discouraged by our historic sufferings that, parrot-like, we repeat and believe these mistakes. Such a one is the assertion that our love of business is extreme. Now it is well known that wherever we are permitted to take part in the uprising of classes, we give up our business as soon as possible. The great majority of Jewish business men give their sons a superior education. Hence, indeed, the so-called "Judaising" of good professions. But even in economically feebler grades of society, our love of trade is not so predominant as is generally supposed. In the Eastern countries of Europe there are great numbers of Jews who are not traders, and who are not afraid of hard work either. The Society of Jews will be in a position to prepare scientifically accurate statistics of our human forces. The new duties and prospects which the new country offers to our people will satisfy our present handicraftsmen, and will transform many present small traders into manual workers.

A pedlar who travels about the country with a heavy pack on his back is not so contented as his persecutors imagine. The seven-hours day will convert all of his kind into workmen. They are brave, misunderstood people, who now suffer perhaps more severely than any others. The Society of Jews will moreover busy itself from the outset with their training as artisans. Their love of gain will be encouraged in wholesome fashion. Jews are of saving and adaptable disposition, and are possessed of strong family feeling. Such people are qualified for any means of earning a living, and it will therefore suffice to make small trading unremunerative, to cause even present pedlars to give it up altogether. This could be brought about, for example, by encouraging large trading-houses which provide all necessaries of life. These general trading-houses are already crushing small trading in capital towns. In the land of new civilization they will absolutely prevent its existence. The establishment of these trading-houses is further advantageous, because it makes the country immediately habitable for people who require more refined necessaries of life.

HABITS.

Is a reference to the little habits and comforts of the ordinary man, in character with the serious nature of this pamphlet?

I think it is in character, and, moreover, very important. For these little habits are the thousand and one fine delicate threads which together go to make up an unbreakable rope.

Here certain limited notions must be set aside. Whoever has seen anything of the world knows that just these little daily customs can easily be transplanted everywhere. The technical contrivances of our day, which this scheme intends to employ in the service of humanity, have heretofore been principally used for our little habits. There are English hotels in Egypt and on the mountain-crests of Switzerland, Vienna cafes in South Africa, French theatres in Russia, German operas in America, and best Bavarian beer in Paris.

When we journey out of Egypt again, we shall not leave the fleshpots behind.

Every man will find his customs again in the local groups, but they will be better, more beautiful, and more agreeable than before.

SOCIETY OF JEWS AND JEWISH STATE

NEGOTIORUM GESTIO.

THIS pamphlet is not intended for lawyers. I can therefore only touch cursorily, as I have so often done, upon my theory of the legal basis of a State.

I must, nevertheless, lay some stress on my new theory, which could be maintained, I believe, even in discussion with men well versed in jurisprudence.

According to Rousseau's now antiquated view, a State is formed by a social contract. Rousseau held that: "The conditions of this contract are so precisely defined by the nature of the agreement that the slightest alteration would make them null and void. The consequence is that, even where they are not expressly stated, they are everywhere identical, and everywhere tacitly accepted and recognized," etc.

A logical and historic refutation of Rousseau's theory was never, nor is now, difficult, however terrible and far-reaching its effects may have been. The question whether a social contract with "conditions not expressly stated, yet unalterable," existed before the framing of a constitution, is a question of little actual interest to States under modern forms of government. The legal relationship between government and citizen is in any case clearly established now.

But previous to the framing of a constitution, and during the creation of a new State, these principles assume great practical importance. We know and see for ourselves that States still continue to be created. Colonies secede from the mother country. Vassals fall away from their suzerain; newly opened territories are immediately formed into free States. It is true that the Jewish

State is conceived as a peculiarly modern structure on unspecified territory. But a State is formed, not by pieces of land, but rather by a number of men united under sovereign rule.

Man is the human, land the objective, groundwork of a State; the human basis being the more important of the two. One supremacy, for example, which has no objective basis at all is perhaps more respected than any in the world, and this is the supremacy of the Pope.

The theory of rationality is the one at present accepted in political science. This theory suffices to justify the creation of a State, and cannot be historically refuted in the same way as the theory of a contract. In so far as I am concerned only with the creation of a Jewish State, I am well within the limits of the theory of rationality. But when I touch upon the legal basis of the State, I have exceeded them. The theories of a Divine institution, or of superior power, or of a contract, and the patriarchal and patrimonial theories do not respond to modern views. The legal basis of a State is sought either too much within men (patriarchal theory, and theories of superior force and contract), or too far above them (Divine institution), or too far below them (objective patrimonial theory). The theory of rationality leaves this question conveniently and carefully unanswered. But a question which has seriously occupied doctors of jurisprudence in every age cannot be an absolutely idle one. As a matter of fact, a mixture of human and superhuman goes to the making of a State. Some legal basis is indispensable to explain the somewhat oppressive relationship in which subjects occasionally stand to rulers. I believe it is to be found in the "negotiorum gestio," wherein the body of citizens represent the dominus negotiorum, and the government represents the gestor.

The Romans, with their marvellous sense of justice, produced that noble masterpiece, the negotiorum gestio. When the property of an oppressed person is in danger, any man may step forward to save it. This man is the gestor, the director of affairs not strictly his own. He has received no warrant—that is, no human warrant—higher obligations authorize him to act. The higher obligations may be formulated in different ways: firstly, for the State; and secondly, so as to respond to individual degrees of culture attained

Society of Jews and Jewish State

by a growing general power of comprehension. The gestio is intended to work for the good of the dominus—the people, to whom the gestor himself belongs.

The gestor administrates property of which he is joint-owner. His joint proprietorship teaches him what urgency would warrant his intervention, and would demand his leadership in peace or war; but under no circumstances is his authority valid *qua* joint proprietorship. The consent of the numerous joint-owners is even under most favorable conditions a matter of conjecture.

A State is created by a nation's struggle for existence. In any such struggle it is impossible to obtain proper authority in circumstantial fashion beforehand. In fact, any previous attempt to obtain a regular decree from the majority would probably ruin the undertaking from the outset. For internal schisms would make the people defenceless against external dangers. We cannot all be of one mind; the gestor will therefore simply take the leadership into his hands and march in the van.

The action of the gestor of the State is sufficiently warranted if the common cause is in danger, and the dominus is prevented, either by want of will or by some other reason, from helping itself.

But the gestor identifies himself with the people by his intervention, and is bound by the agreement *quasi ex contractu*. This is the legal relationship existing before, or, more correctly, created simultaneously with the State.

The gestor thus becomes answerable for every form of negligence, even for the failure of business undertakings, and the neglect of such affairs as are intimately connected with them, etc. I shall not further enlarge on the negotiorum gestio, but rather leave it to the State, else it would take us too far from the main subject. One remark only: "A conducting of affairs with the approbation of the man of business is just as effectual as if it had originally been carried on by his authority."

And how does all this affect our case?

The Jewish people are at present prevented by the diaspora from undertaking the management of their business for themselves. At the present time they are in a condition of more or less severe distress in many parts of the world. They need, above all things, a gestor.

THE JEWISH STATE

This gestor cannot, of course, be a single individual. Such a one would either make himself ridiculous, or—seeing that he would appear to be working for his own interests—contemptible.

The gestor of the Jews must therefore be a body corporate.

And that is the Society of Jews.

THE GESTOR OF THE JEWS.

This medium of the national movement, the nature and functions of which we are at last touching upon, will, in fact, be created before everything else. Its formation is perfectly simple. It will take shape among those energetic Jews to whom I imparted my scheme in London.*

The Society of Jews is the point of departure for the whole Jewish movement about to begin.

The Society will have work to do in the domains of science and politics, for the founding of a Jewish State, as I conceive it, presupposes the application of scientific methods. We cannot journey out of Mizraim today in the primitive fashion of ancient times. We shall previously obtain an accurate account of our number and strength. The Society will be the new Moses of the Jews. The undertaking of that great and ancient gestor of the Jews in primitive days bears much the same relation to ours that an old opera bears to a modern one. We are playing the same melody with many more violins, flutes, harps, violoncellos, and bass-viols; with electric light, decorations, choirs, beautiful costumes, and with the first singers of their day.

This pamphlet is intended to open a general discussion on the Jewish Question. Friends and enemies will take part in it; but it will no longer, I hope, take the form of violent abuse or of sentimental vindication, but of a debate, practical, large, earnest and political.

The Society of Jews will gather all available information from statesmen, Parliaments, Jewish communities; from speeches,

---

* This refers to certain members of the Maccabæans, an organization which, three months after the publication of this pamphlet, rejected his proposals.

Society of Jews and Jewish State

letters and meetings, newspapers and books.

Thus the Society will find out for the first time whether the Jews really wish to go to the Promised Land, and whether they ought to go there. Every Jewish community in the world will send contributions to the Society towards a comprehensive collection of Jewish statistics.

Further tasks, such as investigation by experts of the new country and its natural resources, planning of joint migration and settlement, preliminary work for legislation and administration, etc., must be judiciously evolved out of the original scheme.

Externally, the Society will attempt, as I explained before in the general part, to be acknowledged as a State-forming power. The free assent of many Jews will confer on it the requisite authority in its relations with Governments.

Internally, that is to say, in its relations with the Jewish people, I the Society will create all the first indispensable institutions; it will be the nucleus out of which the public organizations of the Jewish State will later on be developed.

Our first object is, as I said before, supremacy, assured to us by international law, over a portion of the globe sufficiently large to satisfy our just requirements.

What is the next step?

THE OCCUPATION OF LAND.

When nations wandered in historic days they let chance carry them, draw them, fling them hither and thither, and like swarms of locusts they settled down indifferently anywhere. For in historic days the earth was not known to man. But this modern Jewish migration must proceed in accordance with scientific principles.

Not more than forty years ago gold-digging was carried on in an extraordinarily primitive fashion. What adventurous days were those in California! A report brought desperadoes together from every quarter of the earth; they stole pieces of land, robbed each other of gold, and finally gambled it away, as robbers do.

And today! What is gold-digging like in the Transvaal today? Adventurous vagabonds are not there; sedate geologists and engineers alone are on the spot to regulate its gold industry, and

THE JEWISH STATE

to employ ingenious machinery in separating the ore from surrounding rock. Little is left to chance now.

Thus we must investigate and take possession of the new Jewish country by means of every modern expedient.

As soon as we have secured the land we shall send over a ship, having on board the representatives of the Society, of the Company, and of the local groups, who will enter into possession at once.

These men will have three tasks to perform: (1) An accurate, scientific investigation of all natural resources of the country; (2) The organization of a strictly centralized administration; (3) The distribution of land. These tasks intersect one another, and will all be carried out in conformity with the now familiar object in view.

One thing remains to be explained—namely, how the occupation of land according to local groups is to take place.

In America the occupation of newly opened territory is set about in most naive fashion. The settlers assemble on the frontier, and at the appointed time make a simultaneous and violent rush for their portions.

We shall not proceed thus in the new land of the Jews. The lots in provinces and towns will be sold by auction, and paid for, not in money, but in work. The general plan will have settled on streets, bridges, waterworks, etc., necessary for traffic. These will be united into provinces. Within these provinces sites for towns will be similarly sold by auction. The local groups will pledge themselves to carry the business through properly and will pay expenses out of the funds provided for their self-government. The Society will be in a position to judge whether the local groups are not venturing on sacrifices too great for their means. Great commonwealths keep up great scenes of activity. Great sacrifices will thus be rewarded by the establishment of universities, technical schools, academies, etc., and these Government institutions will not be concentrated in the capital, but distributed over the country.

The personal interests of the buyers, and, if necessary, the local authorities, will guarantee the proper working of what has been taken over. In the same way as we cannot, and indeed do not wish to, obliterate distinctions between single individuals, so the differences between local groups will also continue to be marked.

Society of Jews and Jewish State

Everything will shape itself quite naturally. All acquired rights will be protected, and every new development will be given sufficient scope.

Our people will be made thoroughly acquainted with all these matters.

We shall not take others unawares or mislead them, any more than we shall deceive ourselves.

Everything must be systematically settled beforehand. I merely indicate this scheme, our acutest thinkers will combine in elaborating it. Every sociological and technical acquirement of our age, and of the more advanced age which will be reached before the slow execution of my plan is accomplished, must be employed for this object. Every valuable invention that exists now, or lies in the future, must be used. By these means a country can be occupied and a State founded in a manner as yet unknown to history, and with possibilities of success such as never occurred before.

CONSTITUTION.

One of the great committees which the Society will have to appoint will be the council of jurists of the State. These must formulate the best, that is, the best modern constitution possible. I believe that a good constitution should be of moderately elastic nature. In another work I have explained in detail what forms of government I hold to be the best. I think a democratic monarchy and an aristocratic republic are the two most superior forms of a State, because in them the form of State and the principle of government are opposed to one another, and thus preserve a true balance of power. I am a staunch supporter of monarchical institutions, because these allow of a consistent policy, and represent the interests of a historically famous family born and educated to rule, whose desires are bound up with the preservation of the State. But our history has been too long interrupted for us to attempt direct continuity of ancient constitutional forms without exposing ourselves to the charge of absurdity.

A democracy without a sovereign's useful counterpoise is extreme in appreciation and condemnation, tends to idle discussion

THE JEWISH STATE

of different creeds and different nationalities came to live amongst us, we should accord them honorable protection, and equality before the law. We learnt toleration in Europe. This is not sarcastically said; for the Anti-Semitism of today could in very few places be taken for old religious intolerance. It is for the most part a movement among civilized nations by which they try to chase away the spectres of their own past.

LAWS.

When the idea of a State begins to approach realization, the Society of Jews will appoint a council of jurists to do the preparatory work of legislation. During the transition period these must act on the principle that every emigrant Jew is to be judged according to the laws of the country which he has left. But they must try to bring about a unification of these various laws to form a modern system of legislation based on the best portions of previous systems. This might become a typical codification, responsive to all the just social claims of the present day.

THE ARMY.

The Jewish State is conceived as a neutral one. It will therefore require only an army of volunteers, equipped, of course, with every requisite of modern warfare, to preserve order internally and externally.

THE BANNER.*

We have no banner, and we need one. If we desire to lead men forward, we must raise an emblem above their heads.

I would suggest a white banner, bearing seven golden stars. The white field symbolizing our pure new life; the seven stars, the seven golden hours of our working-day. For we shall march into the Promised Land carrying the badge of labor.

---

* This badge bad vogue at the first Congress. The blue and white, with the Shield of David, has been generally accepted, and was designed in 1880.

Society of Jews and Jewish State

RECIPROCITY AND CARTELS.

The Jewish State must be properly founded, with due regard to our future honorable position in the world. Therefore every obligation in the old country must be scrupulously fulfilled before leaving. The Society of Jews and Jewish Company will grant cheap passage and certain advantages in settlement to those only who can present an official testimonial from their local authorities, certifying that they have left their affairs in good order.

Every just private claim originating in the abandoned countries will be heard more readily in the Jewish State than anywhere else. We shall not wait for reciprocity; we shall act purely for the sake of our own honor. We shall thus perhaps find, later on, that strange law courts will be more willing to hear our claims than now seems to be the case in some places.

It will be inferred, as a matter of course, from foregone remarks, that we shall deliver up Jewish criminals more readily than any other State would do, till the time comes when we can enforce our penal code on the same principles as every other civilized nation does. There will therefore be a period of transition, during which we shall receive our criminals only after they have suffered due penalties. But, having made amends, they will be received without any restrictions whatever, for our criminals also must enter upon a new life.

Thus emigration may become to many Jews a crisis with a happy issue. Bad external circumstances, which ruin many a character, will be removed, and this change may mean salvation to many who are lost.

Here I should like briefly to relate a story I came across in an account of the gold mines of Witwatersrand. One day a man came to the rand, settled there, tried his hand at various things, with the exception of gold-mining, till he founded an ice factory, which did well. He won universal esteem by his respectability, till one day he was suddenly arrested. He had committed some defalcations as banker in Frankfort, had fled from there, and had begun a new life under an assumed name. But when he was led away as prisoner, the chief local dignitaries appeared at the station, bade him a cordial farewell, and au revoir!—for he was certain to return.

What does not this story reveal! A new life can regenerate even criminals, and we have a proportionately small number of these. Some interesting statistics on this point are worth reading, entitled, "The Criminality of Jews in Germany," by Dr. P. Nathan, of Berlin, who was commissioned by the "Society for Defence against Anti-Semitism" to make a collection of statistics based on official returns. It is true that this pamphlet, which teems with figures, arises, as does many another "defence," out of the error that Anti-Semitism can be subdued by reasonable arguments. We are probably disliked as much for our gifts as we are for our faults.

BENEFITS OF THE IMMIGRATION OF THE JEWS.

I imagine that Governments will, either voluntarily or under pressure from the Anti-Semites, pay certain attention to this scheme; and they may perhaps actually receive it here and there with a sympathy which they will also show to the Society of Jews.

For the emigration which I suggest will not create any economic crises. Such crises as would follow everywhere in consequence of Jew-baiting would rather be prevented by the carrying out of my plan. A great period of prosperity would commence in countries which are now Anti-Semitic. For there will be, as I have repeatedly said, an intermigration of Christian citizens into the positions slowly and systematically evacuated by the Jews. If we are not merely suffered, but actually assisted to do this, the movement will have a generally beneficial effect. That is a narrow view which sees in the departure of many Jews a consequent impoverishment of countries. Different is a departure which is a result of persecution, for here property is indeed destroyed, as it is ruined in the confusion of war. Different again is the peaceable voluntary departure of colonists, wherein everything is carried out with due consideration for acquired rights, and with absolute conformity to law, openly and by light of day, under the supervision of authority and the control of public opinion. The emigration of Christian proletariats to different parts of the world would be definitely brought to a standstill by the Jewish movement.

The States would have a further advantage in the enormous increase of their export trade; for, since the emigrant Jews "over

Society of Jews and Jewish State

there" would depend for a long time to come on European productions, the States would necessarily have to provide them. The local groups would keep up a just balance, and the customary needs would have to be supplied for a long time at the accustomed places.

Another, and perhaps one of the greatest advantages, would be the ensuing social relief. Social dissatisfaction would be appeased during the twenty or more years which the emigration of the Jews would occupy, and would in any case be set at rest during the whole transition period.

The shape which the social question may take depends entirely on the development of our technical contrivances. Steam-power concentrated men in factories about machinery, where they were over-crowded, and where they made one another miserable by over-crowding. Our present enormous, injudicious and unsystematic rate of production is the cause of continual severe crises which ruin both managers and employés. Steam crowded men together; electricity will probably scatter them again, and may perhaps bring about a more prosperous condition of the labor market. In any case, our scientific discoverers, who are the true benefactors of humanity, will continue their labors after the commencement of the emigration of the Jews, and they will discover things as marvellous as those we have already seen, or indeed more wonderful even than these.

The word "impossible" has ceased to exist for our men of science. Were a man who lived in the last century to return to the earth, he would find the life of today full of incomprehensible magic. Wherever we moderns appear with our inventions, we transform the desert into a garden. To build a city takes in our time as many years as it formerly required centuries; America offers endless examples of this. Distance has ceased to be an obstacle. The spirit of our age has gathered fabulous treasures into its storehouse. Every day this wealth increases. A hundred thousand heads are occupied with speculations and research at every point of the globe, and the discovery of one becomes, ere long, the property of the whole world. We ourselves will use and carry on every new attempt in our Jewish State; we shall Introduce the seven-hours day as an experiment for the good of humanity; and we shall proceed in everything else in the same humane spirit, making of the new land a land of experiments and a model State.

The undertakings made by the Jews will remain, after their managers' departure, where they originally were founded. And the Jewish spirit of enterprise will not even fail there where people welcome it. For Jewish capitalists will be glad to invest their funds where they are familiar with surrounding conditions. And whereas Jewish money is now sent out of countries on account of existing persecutions, and is sunk in most distant foreign undertakings, it will flow back again in consequence of this peaceable solution, and will help further to raise the status of the countries which the Jews have left.

CONCLUSION

HOW MUCH has been left unexplained, how many defects, how many regrettable signs of carelessness, how many useless repetitions, in the pamphlet which I have so long considered and so carefully revised!

But a fair-minded reader, who has sufficient understanding to grasp the spirit of my words, will not be repelled by these defects. He will rather be roused thereby to devote his intelligence and energy to the improvement of a work which is not one man's task alone.

Have I not explained obvious things and overlooked important considerations?

I have tried to meet certain objections; but I know that many more will be made, based on high grounds and low.

To the first class of objections belongs the remark, that the Jews are not the only people in the world who are in a condition of distress. Here I would reply that we may as well begin by removing some of this misery, even it it should at first be no more than our own.

It might further be said that we ought not to create distinctions between people; we ought not to raise fresh barriers; we should rather make the old disappear. But men who think in this way are amiable visionaries; and the idea of a native land will still flourish when the dust of their bones will have vanished tracelessly in the winds. Universal brotherhood is not even a beautiful dream. Antagonism is essential to man's greatest efforts.

But the Jews, once settled in their own State, would probably have no more enemies, and since prosperity enfeebles and causes them to diminish, they would soon disappear altogether. I think the Jews will always have sufficient enemies, much as every other nation has. But once fixed on their own land, it will no longer be possible for them to scatter all over the world. The diaspora cannot take place again, unless the civilization of the whole earth is destroyed; and such a consummation could be feared by none but foolish men. Our present civilization possesses weapons powerful enough for its self-defence.

Innumerable objections will be based on low grounds, for there are more low men than noble in this world. I have tried to remove some of these narrow-minded notions; and whoever is willing to fall in behind our white flag with its seven golden stars must assist in this campaign of enlightenment. Perhaps we shall have to fight first of all against many an evil-disposed, narrow-hearted, short-sighted member of our own race.

Again, people will say that I am furnishing the Anti-Semites with weapons. Why so? Because I admit the truth? Because I do not maintain that there are none but excellent men amongst us?

Again, people will say that I am showing our enemies the way to injure us. This I absolutely dispute. My proposal could only be carried out with the free consent of a majority of Jews. Individuals or even powerful bodies of Jews might be attacked, but Governments will take no action against the collective nation. The equal rights of Jews before the law cannot be withdrawn where they have once been conceded; for the first attempt at withdrawal would immediately drive all Jews, rich and poor alike, into the ranks of the revolutionary party. The first official violation of Jewish liberties invariably brings about an economic crisis. Therefore no weapons can be effectually used against us, because these cut the hands that wield them. Meantime hatred grows apace. The rich do not feel it much, but our poor do. Let us ask our poor, who have been more severely persecuted since the last renewal of Anti-Semitism than ever before.

Our prosperous men may say that the pressure is not yet severe enough to justify emigration, and that every forcible expulsion shows how unwilling our people are to depart. True, because they do not know where to go; because they only pass from one trouble into another. But we are showing them the way to the Promised Land; and the splendid force of enthusiasm must fight against the terrible force of habit.

Conclusion

Persecutions are no longer so malignant as they were in the Middle Ages. True, but our sensitiveness has increased, so that we feel no diminution in our sufferings; endless persecution has overstrained our nerves.

Will people say, again, that our enterprise is hopeless, because even if we obtained the land with supremacy over it, the poor only would go with us? It is precisely the poorest whom we need at first. Only desperadoes make good conquerors.

Will some one say, Were it feasible, it would have been done long ago?

It has never yet been possible; now it is possible. A hundred, or even fifty years ago, it would have been nothing more than a dream. Today it may become a reality. Our rich, who have a pleasurable acquaintance with all our technical acquisitions, know full well how much money can do. And thus it will be: just the poor and simple, who do not know what power man already exercises over the forces of nature, just these will have firmest faith in the new message; for these have never lost their hope of the Promised Land.

Here it is, fellow-Jews! Neither fable nor fraud! Every man may test its reality for himself, for every man will carry with him a portion of the Promised Land—one in his head, another in his arms, another in his acquired possessions.

Now all this may appear to be an interminably long affair. Even under favorable circumstances many years might elapse before the commencement of the foundation of the State. Meantime, Jews in a hundred different places would suffer insults, mortification, abuse, blows, depredation and death. Not so, the initial steps towards the execution of the plan would stop Anti-Semitism at once and for ever. Ours is a treaty of peace.

The news of the formation of our Jewish Company will be carried in a single day to the remotest ends of the earth by the lightning speed of our telegraph wires.

And immediate relief will ensue. The mediocre intellects which we produce so superabundantly in our middle classes will find an outlet in our first organizations, as our first scientists, officers, professors, officials, lawyers, and doctors, and thus the movement will continue in swift but smooth progression.

Prayers will be offered up for the success of our work in temples and in churches also; for it will bring ease from a burden which has long weighed on all men.

But we must first bring enlightenment to men's minds. The idea must make its way into the most distant, miserable holes where our people dwell. They will awaken from gloomy brooding, for into their lives will come a new significance. If every man thinks only of himself, what vast proportions the movements will assume!

And what glory awaits those who fight unselfishly for the cause!

Therefore I believe that a wonderous generation of Jews will spring into existence. The Maccabæans will rise again.

Let me repeat once more my opening words: The Jews wish to have a State, and they shall have one.

We shall live at last as free men on our own soil, and die peacefully in our own home.

The world will be freed by our liberty, enriched by our wealth, magnified by our greatness.

And whatever we attempt there to accomplish for our own welfare will react with beneficent force for the good of humanity.

Visit us at *www.quidprobooks.com.*

www.ingramcontent.com/pod-product-compliance
Lightning Source LLC
Chambersburg PA
CBHW051657040426
42446CB00009B/1184